PROBLEMS OF DEATH DEATH DEATH DEATH DEATH DEATI DEATI DEA

OPPOSING VIEWPOINTS

DAVID L. BENDER
Editor

GREENHAVEN PRESS — ANOKA, MINNESOTA 55303

© Copyright 1974 by Greenhaven Press

ISBN 0-912616-13-X Paper Edition
ISBN 0-912616-32-6 Cloth Edition

TABLE OF CONTENTS

TABLE OF CONTENTS

TABLE OF EXERCISES

A major emphasis of this book is on critical thinking skills. Discussion exercises included after readings are not laborious writing assignments. They are included to stimulate class discussion and individual critical thinking.

ABORTION

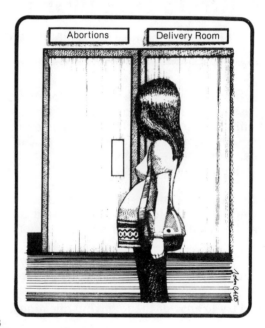

Readings

ABORTION IS OUR RIGHT

The Boston Women's Health Book Collective

The Boston Women's Health Book Collective began as a discussion group on "women and their bodies." It evolved into a course for women and eventually the course outline and notes were published as **Our Bodies Ourselves**. The theme of the book is that it is for women, about women and by women.

The Collective is made up of twelve women who range in age from 24 to 40, some married and some single, with varied educational and professional backgrounds.

As you read try to answer the following questions:

1. How does the reading respond to the objection that abortion violates the natural law?
2. What is quickening? How does it relate to the law and abortion?
3. According to this reading abortion became a crime in the U.S. in the last century for three reasons. What were those reasons?

Boston Women's Health Book Collective, **Our Bodies Ourselves** (New York: Simon and Schuster, 1973), pp. 138-53. Copyright © 71, 1973, by the Boston Women's Health Book Collective. Reprinted by permission of Simon and Schuster.

Abortion is our right — our right as women to control our bodies. In almost every community in this country a woman with an unwanted pregnancy is frustrated and obstructed by laws, hospitals, doctors, by high prices and poor communications. The same public whose sex-filled media urge her to be sexy turns on her with moralistic disapproval that isolates her and forces her to deal with her problem in secret. Some strong and concerned people have changed a few state laws and started some good abortion-referral services and humane clinics, but for too many American women legal abortions are hard to get, hard to pay for, and once gotten, are alienating and lonely experiences. ...

History of Abortion

One of the myths that antiabortionists use to influence legislators and to harass and scare the woman with an unwanted pregnancy is that abortion violates some age-old and God-given natural law. One look at history shows that they are lying or terribly misled. Until one hundred years ago almost no one — not even the Catholic Church — punished abortion in the early stages of pregnancy. Lawrence Lader says that ''the Greek city states and ancient Rome, the foundations of Western civilization, made abortion the basis of a well-ordered population policy'' (**Abortion**, p. 76). Christianity infused the fetus with a soul, but during eighteen centuries of debate the Church took the' conveniently loose view that the fetus became animated by the rational soul, and abortion was therefore a serious crime, only at forty days after conception for a boy and eighty days for a girl. (No methods of sex determination were specified.) English common law by the thirteenth century settled into a fairly tolerant acceptance of abortion up until quickening, the unspecific moment, usually in the fifth month, when the woman feels the fetus move. In the United States for a long time the common law inherited from England protected the right of abortion in early pregnancy.

Suddenly in the nineteenth century things tightened up. In 1869 Pope Pius IX eliminated the distinction between an animated and nonanimated fetus, and since then the Catholic Church has called all abortion murder and punished it severely. Antiabortion laws were first passed in England in 1803 and became stricter through the century. Connecticut in 1821 punished abortion of a fetus by poison after it had quickened, but as in other states, a succession of laws followed which culminated around 1860 in outlawing all abortions except those ''necessary to save the life of the woman.''

3

SOCIETY AND CHURCHES HAVE
NOT CONSIDERED RIGHTS OF WOMEN

In determining their positions on abortion, society and the churches traditionally have not given sufficient consideration to the rights and desires of women. Historically, in the Western world, it has been men who have made the decision whether or not abortion is to be sanctioned. Early in history, men were assumed to be the only legal parent. Even in the nineteenth century it was believed by many that the sperm was a miniature baby that was placed in the woman to be nourished. The man's rights were supreme. The woman was subject first to father and then to husband. Her life was circumscribed by sexual and procreative purposes. According to this view, her sexuality was essentially locked into child-bearing and child-rearing.

Even today, most of society considers every child primarily the responsibility of a woman for seventeen to twenty years in terms of personal care and commitment of time, energy and emotional involvement. While the churches and society may impose sanctions on a woman and require her to carry through an unintended or problem pregnancy, they provide her with little continuing support for the seventeen to twenty years of child-rearing. In fact, women and children are more likely to face a strong set of obstacles which are detrimental to them.

From **Abortion: A Paper For Study** by a task force appointed by the National Council of Churches.

There were three main reasons why abortion suddenly became a "crime." The first was quite decent: abortion until recently was a dangerous operation — methods crude, antiseptics scarce, even hospitals dirty. It was in part the mid-nineteenth-century wave of humanitarianism that pressed for abortion laws to protect women. The second motive of the antiabortionists was less laudable. As biologists in the nineteenth century began to understand conception, women began to practice more effective contraception. Catholic

4

countries such as France began "losing" the population race, and the Church wanted to keep its mothers in the running. So the Church itself turned to biology and used the idea that "life" and therefore soul-infused human life, begins at fertilization. This reasoning also spread to England and the United States. At that time English and American industries needed workers, the huge farmable territories of the new world needed farmers, and the Civil War had depleted America's labor crop. Abortion laws saw to it that woman took her place beside the other machines of a developing economy.

The third reason for the sudden emergence of anti-abortion laws is the most dangerous: it is the idea that sex for pleasure is bad, that pregnancy is a punishment for pleasure, and that fear of pregnancy will reinforce "degenerating" modern morals. These ideas had long fought for supremacy in the Catholic Church, and showed in 1869 that they had won. The English and American puritanism which still perverts our minds flourished in the nineteenth century; it is significant that the 1873 U.S. federal law that banned from the mails any literature, medicine, or article to do with contraception or abortion was engineered and executed by Anthony Comstock, fanatical secretary of the New York Society for the Prevention of Vice. Today the idea that sex is bad is used with cruel sadism on the victim of an unwanted pregnancy by her community and, worse, by her doctors, many of whom underneath it all feel that a little humiliation and a little pain might teach a girl a lesson. It is partly this thinking that slows down the development of quick and painless methods of abortion. And in a majority of states, including Massachusetts, puritanism still works to keep abortion laws and practices rigid. Undaunted by Prohibition, the legislators of morality cannot stop sex, but yearly send many American women hundreds of miles for legal abortions or, if they are unlucky, underground for dangerous and often fatal criminal abortions. ...

JANUARY, 1973

The landmark decision of the Supreme Court in January, 1973, has radically changed the abortion situation in this country. The Supreme Court now affirms that the "right of privacy...founded in the 14th Amendment's concept of personal liberty...is broad enough to encompass a woman's decision whether or not to terminate her pregnancy." Specifically the Court held that up to the first trimester of pregnancy, the decision to have an abortion may be made solely by the pregnant woman and her doctor. Following approximately the end of the first trimester, a state's power to regulate abortion is limited to the establishment of rules governing where and by whom an abortion may be performed. "It is only when the fetus has reached a point of viability (from 24 to 28 weeks of gestation) that the state may go so far as to proscribe abortion...except when it is necessary to preserve the life or health of the mother."

ABORTION VIOLATES THE SACREDNESS OF HUMAN LIFE

James P. Shannon

James P. Shannon is currently an attorney in Albuquerque, New Mexico. He also teaches a course in the legal profession at the University of New Mexico law school. He is a former Catholic priest and auxiliary bishop of St. Paul, Minnesota. He has published numerous articles in various Catholic publications and has an extensive educational background both as a student and teacher.

Reflect on the following questions while you read:

1. What was the Supreme Court's decision in the case of Roe v. Wade on January 22, 1973?
2. Why does Mr. Shannon feel that abortion within three months of conception is not a morally neutral act?
3. What conclusion has Mr. Shannon reached as a result of counseling women who have had abortions?

From James P. Shannon's weekly column "The Pilgrim Church," **The Minneapolis Tribune**, February 18 and 25, 1973. Reprinted with permission from **The Minneapolis Tribune**.

Few decisions of the Supreme Court have ever been simultaneously praised and denounced as enthusiastically as that handed down by the court Jan. 22 in the decision styled Roe vs. Wade. By a vote of 7 to 2, with Justices White and Rehnquist dissenting, the court struck down as unconstitutional any state law that denies a pregnant woman the right to an abortion during the first three months (first trimester) of her pregnancy.

Proponents of abortion have praised the Supreme Court for the wisdom and the courage of its decision. And right-to-life committees, organized in most states, have promptly announced plans to fight the Supreme Court decision by a massive campaign of political pressure, directed at the court, the Congress and the President. Saying that they speak for the human rights of the unborn, these committees are convinced that a human person exists in the womb of a mother from the moment of conception.

Writing for the majority of the court in Roe, Justice Blackmun says: "We need not resolve the difficult question of when life begins. When those trained in the respective disciplines of medicine, philosophy and theology are unable to arrive at any consensus, the judiciary, at this point in the development of man's knowledge, is not in a position to speculate as to the answer."

Critics of the majority opinion quickly respond that the question of when life begins in the human fetus is precisely the critical question and that it cannot be side-stepped by the court simply by admitting that it is a tough question.

Writing in dissent for the minority, Justice White said: "I find nothing in the language or history of the Constitution to support the court's judgment. The court simply fashions and announces a new constitutional right for pregnant mothers and, with scarcely any reason or authority for its action, invests that right with sufficient substance to override most existing state abortion statutes."

It is worth noting that the opinion of the majority spends an unusually large amount of space discussing the medical, ethical and legislative history of deliberate abortion. It almost seems that the majority rests its case on a lack of consensus among professionals in disciplines outside the law and then proceeds to build on this shaky foundation in new principles of law.

> **It seems to me as clear as daylight that abortion would be a crime.**

Mahatma Gandhi

I would defend, without endorsing, the majority opinion on the ground that both sides in this perennial debate ultimately rest their case on premises of belief that neither one can prove scientifically or with finality.

The pro-abortionists believe that the human fetus is not a human person (in the sense that the term is used in the 14th Amendment) until it is capable of living outside the womb.

The anti-abortionists believe that the human fetus, from the moment of conception, is indeed a human person, with all the constitutional rights assured to other human persons. I confess that I share this opinion.

I do admit, however, that it is an opinion. I think I can give several reasonable arguments in support of it. However, to share this fundamental belief with other persons does not mean that I endorse the current political campaigns to amend the Constitution, to reprove the Supreme Court or to devise new state laws prohibiting abortion.

Quite the contrary. I have said more than once, and I now repeat the opinion, that the decision to perform an abortion should be a moral and medical judgment made in good conscience by a pregnant woman and her doctor.

To say that is certainly not to endorse the concept of "abortion on demand." In fact, I consider the deliberate taking of a human fetus from the body of a mother-to-be an act of violence. It seems to me to be a deliberate violation of nature, even though I admit there are circumstances in which it might be justified.

9

I believe that one fuzzy conclusion reached by many pro-abortionists who read the Supreme Court decision carelessly is that deliberate abortion within three months of conception is simply a morally neutral act. I would argue that the fetus, whether person or non-person at that time, has an identity, integrity, sacredness and potentiality which should not be promiscuously abused or denied.

Editorializing in the Christian Century, J. Claude Evans urges that "pro-abortionists and anti-abortionists...unite on taking the matter of abortion out of the statute books altogether." Although my premises are not precisely those of Evans, I find it easily possible to concur wholeheartedly in the reasonableness of his final proposal on abortion.

These are his words: "About all we need on the statute book is some limiting law — perhaps stating that no abortions are permitted beyond 18-week gestation and protecting the right of any doctor or hospital to refuse to perform abortions on demand. The effect of the destatutizing of abortion would be to show respect for the pluralism of our society. Anti-abortionist individuals and churches would be free to teach their faith views without the onus of a permissive state law that would make their teaching more difficult.

"At the same time, pro-abortionists would also be able to teach their faith views without the support of a state law that would tend to give them the illusion of universality. And the ecumenical community would find itself enriched by the seriousness of communally apprehended standards without leaning on the state to do its dirty work of moral enforcement."

I say "amen" to the Evans proposal. ...

ABORTION FROM THE EMBRYO'S POINT OF VIEW

Look at the question from the point of view of the human embryo. It is a human embryo from the moment the female ovum is fertilized. Allowed to grow to term, it will be a small but fully human person at birth. Its life from conception is a growing continuum. And conversely, if that spark of life be ended before birth, the living entity that ends is more than merely an appendage to the body of the mother.

The Supreme Court...decided that it is now permissible under the law for a pregnant woman and her doctor to terminate life in the womb between the time of conception and a date six months later.

**UNBORN FETUS AT 20 WEEKS
ACTUAL SIZE**

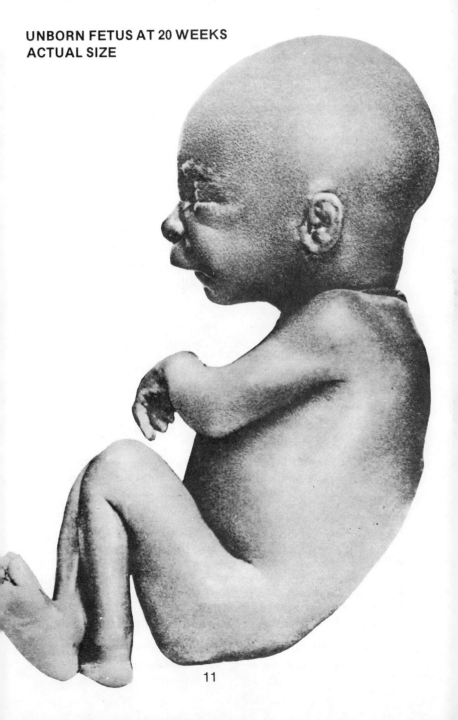

A close reading of the court's opinion would seem to say that the human fetus can not be taken from the mother in the last trimester (three months) of pregnancy, except for certain grave reasons, can readily be taken in the first trimester, and can, under specified conditions, be taken during the middle three months of pregnancy.

Apart from the arithmetical symmetry of those three neat periods of gestation, one seeks in vain in the court's opinion for any substantive reason why the legal rights inhering in the human fetus change quality after 90 days and again after 180 days. What accounts for these changes? And who decides that these changes are sufficient to permit or to ban abortion?

The simple answer for us now is that the Supreme Court has decided. And on what premise? We do not know. Seven of nine justices have declared that what is permissible for six months after conception may be criminally illegal thereafter. And under the law of this nation, that question is settled for the present. It is settled, however, only in the sense that the Supreme Court is, under the Constitution, the final arbiter of the law in our legal system.

If human life is sacred in hospital wards and nurseries, if it is sacred in Death Row at San Quentin and if it is sacred in rest homes for the infirm and elderly, then it must be sacred wherever it exists, inside or outside the womb. Human life is human life from its beginning to its ending.

CONSTITUTIONAL AMENDMENT

"Sec. 1. With respect to the right to life, the word 'person,' as we used in this article and in the 5th and 14th articles of amendments to the constitution of the United States, applies to all human beings, including their unborn offspring at every state of their biological development, irrespective of age, health, function or condition of dependency. Sec. 2. This article shall not apply in an emergency when a reasonable medical certainty exists that continuation of the pregnancy will cause the death of the mother. Sec. 3. Congress and the several states shall have the power to enforce this article by legislation in their appropriate jurisdictions."

Proposed by Senator James Buckley, Conservative, New York State.

ABORTION FROM THE MOTHER'S POINT OF VIEW

Consider abortion from the point of view of ·the mother-to-be. Why, in a given instance, does she wish to terminate her pregnancy? Because she was raped? Because her child may be born deformed? Because she already has too many children? Because she regrets the occasion of conception? Because she cannot psychologically or economically bear the burden of rearing another child?

Each of these reasons, and a host of others, merits careful weighing. Each deserves to be balanced in the scales against the rights that inhere in the unborn human fetus.

If the right to life is sacred, then the right of an unborn child to be born and to grow and to develop his potentialities deserves, at the very least, to be balanced against the psychological, physical, human and economic needs of his mother and family-to-be.

In the current round of public discussion of abortion, many women who are prominent in society have publicly acknowledged that they have obtained abortions recently. They do not argue that they were raped or that they feared their babies would be born deformed. They candidly admit that they got pregnant when they did not wish to do so. Is that a good enough reason for ending the pregnancy? I say it is not.

If a woman believes that her right to control her own body extends always and easily to the violent act of abortion, I respectfully submit that her concern for the integrity of her body should begin at least 91 days before the end of her first trimester of pregnancy. ...

My experience in counseling women who have had abortions, both legally and illegally, leads me to the conclusion that the burdens of bearing a baby to term, even an unwanted or unexpected baby, which is later put up for adoption, are usually far less traumatic than the consequences of deliberate abortion.

I am aware that many regular readers will disagree vehemently with the thesis and the premises for this column. I do not mean to say either that such persons are wrong or that I am right.

I merely offer today, out of "a decent respect for the

13

opinion of mankind,'' some reasons that impel me to believe that abortion is an act of violence and therefore not to be taken lightly in any culture that still professes to base its legal and ethical system on the premise that all human life is sacred.

NO UNWANTED CHILDREN

American Friends Service Committee

The following statement is part of a report made by a Working Party of the American Friends Service Committee because of public concern over abortion. The AFSC asked the Working Party to consider what contribution the thoughts and beliefs of the Society of Friends (Quaker Church) might make to the resolution of the problem. The AFSC is a service arm of the Society of Friends.

Consider the following questions while reading:

1. What is the reasoning behind the Quaker claim that "no woman should be forced to bear an unwanted child"?
2. What more is needed, in the opinion of the authors, than just the repeal of abortion laws?

American Friend's Service Committee, **Who Shall Live? Man's Control Over Birth and Death** (New York: Hill and Wang, 1970), pp. 64-66. Reprinted with the permission of Farrar, Straus & Giroux, Inc. from **Who Shall Live? Man's Control Over Birth and Death** by American Friends Service Committee, Copyright © 1970 by Hill and Wang, Inc.

We believe that no woman should be forced to bear an unwanted child. A woman should be able to have an abortion legally if she has decided that this is the only solution she can accept and if the physician agrees that it is in the best interests of mother and child. She should be encouraged to seek the best social and spiritual counseling available before reaching a decision; and the physician, for his own support, should have the opportunity to confer with colleagues of his choosing if he feels the need for such consultation.

Believing that abortion should be subject to the same regulations and safeguards as those governing other medical and surgical procedures, we urge the repeal of all laws limiting either the circumstances under which a woman may have an abortion or the physician's freedom to use his best professional judgment in performing it.

We believe that no physician should be forced to perform an abortion if this violates his conscience; but, if this is so, he has an obligation to refer his patient to another physician willing to serve her.

We were drawn to these conclusions by facts and considerations that bear repetition.

The need for abortions may be greatly reduced when contraceptives that are as acceptable, effective, and safe as possible become readily available. But until that time, it can be assumed from the evidence that women will continue to have abortions. No prohibitions or penalties anywhere in the world have succeeded in stopping them. Instead, restrictive laws have made them more difficult to obtain, more dangerous, and more degrading.

Current laws in the United States are discriminatory, since the rich find it possible to secure abortions unobtainable by the poor. They promote criminal activity and disrespect for law. They are an invasion of human rights: the right of a child to be wanted and loved, the right of a woman to decide whether and when she will have children. And, by interfering with the right of families to limit the number of their children, present laws contribute to population pressures.

While we found all of the above considerations persuasive and important, the most decisive factors in reaching our conclusions have been our concern that the individual, the family, and society achieve the highest

16

possible quality of life and our conviction that this is unlikely for mentally and physically damaged or unwanted children, for their parents, and for an overpopulated world.

On religious, moral, and humanitarian grounds, therefore, we arrived at the view that it is far better to end an unwanted pregnancy than to encourage the evils resulting from forced pregnancy and childbirth. At the center of our position is a profound respect and reverence for human life, not only that of the potential human being who should never have been conceived, but of the parents, the other children, and the community of man.

Mothering is a task that requires enormous human and emotional resources. It is an obligation that confronts and challenges the woman's capacity to care night and day. When this task is carried out in the spirit of love and fulfillment, it is hard but rewarding work. But when the child is unwanted, the task may become onerous, and the obligations created may become a lifetime sentence, an ordeal emotionally destructive to the mother and disastrous for the child.

The Right To Abortion: A Psychiatric View by the Committee On Psychiatry and Law.

MUCH MORE IS NEEDED

The repeal of abortion laws seems to us to be a step in the right direction, but much more is needed:

1. Positive programs to do away with the necessity for abortions.
2. A program of medically sound and easily available abortion services at low cost to protect women against the health problems resulting from recourse to back-street abortionists.
3. Abortion services as part of accepted medical care, paid for by public funds for those who depend on public funds for such care.

4. Availability of counseling and social services to women requesting abortion with a view to (a) helping them examine the alternatives to abortion, (b) exploring with them sources of aid — medical, financial, adoptive — to make possible carrying the baby to term and rearing it decently, (c) putting them in touch with social services equipped to deal with such other problems as employment and housing, and (d) providing contraceptive advice and education as protection against future unwanted pregnancies. It is society's responsibility to provide such counseling services where they are not now available.

In pursuing these approaches, we must not lose sight of the need to work toward larger goals — raising educational levels and standards of living — important to the quality of life both as ends in themselves and as necessary means of motivating people to control their fertility.

CASE STUDY:
FETAL EXPERIMENTATION

The picture below shows a British doctor at Cambridge University's Department of Experimental Medicine experimenting on a living, legally aborted human fetus. The doctor explains that he is "using something which is destined for the incinerator to benefit mankind."

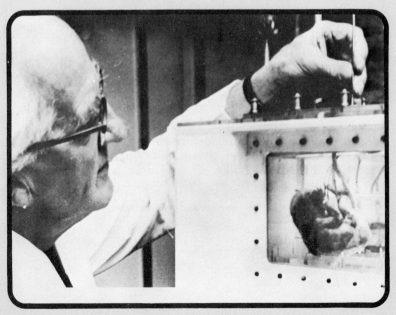

INSTRUCTIONS

Your state legislature is debating a bill that would permit experimentation on aborted fetuses until the 28th week of pregnancy.

STEP 1. The class should break into groups of four to six students.

STEP 2. Each group should pretend it represents a church council with the problem of deciding what position to take on the issue for the purpose of influencing its state senator.

STEP 3. After a majority of the members of each council decide what position to take, the council should be able to present its reasoning to the whole class.

ARGUMENTS FOR FETAL EXPERIMENTATION

1. The fetus has no personality and feelings, and need not be accorded the rights of a human being.
2. Experimentation would benefit all mankind and lessen the suffering of many.
3. One cannot stop the march of progress.

ARGUMENTS AGAINST FETAL EXPERIMENTATION

1. The fetus should be granted the rights due other human persons.
2. Fetal experimentation is worse than murder, and can be compared to torture before execution.
3. Abortion is the best alternative between two negative choices; it should not be worsened by fetal experimentation.

THE ABORTING SOCIETY

by Thomas W. Hilgers, Marjory Mecklenburg and Gayle Riordan

Thomas W. Hilgers is currently a fellow in obstetrics and gynecology at the Mayo Graduate School of Medicine in Rochester, Minnesota. He has authored a number of papers on the subject of abortion and is the co-editor of **Abortion and Social Justice**.

Marjory Mecklenburg is chairwoman of the Problem Pregnancy Research and Advisory Committee of Minnesota. She is also a founding member of Minneapolis Birthright and is the current president of Minnesota Citizens Concerned for Life, Inc.

Gayle Riordan is director of the L.P.N. Nursing Program at St. Mary's School of Nursing in Rochester, Minnesota. She formerly was head nurse in obstetrics at St. Mary's Hospital and a nurse advisor in South Vietnam from 1967 to 1968.

Consider the following questions while reading:

1. The authors claim that members of our affluent society are selfish and unwilling to give of themselves to others. How do they relate this statement to the abortion issue?
2. What is meant by the terms ''social abortion'' and ''self abortion''?

Thomas W. Hilgers, Marjory Mecklenburg and Gayle Rioran, ''Is Abortion The Best We Have To Offer?'' **Abortion and Social Justice**, eds. Thomas W. Hilgers and Dennis J. Horan (New York: Sheed and Ward, 1972), pp. 177-97. Copyright 1972, Thomas W. Hilgers and Dennis J. Horan. Published by Sheed and Ward.

Why does a "civilized" society become so threatened by its own offspring that it seeks the violence of human abortion to relieve its anxiety? Why do innocent children become such a threat that parents are moved to destroy them? Why does a society which attempts to promote peace and justice continue to advocate the mass slaughter of unborn children? These questions are not easy for anyone to answer. And yet, that alone does not detract from the reality of their implication: the reality of a society which is rapidly engulfing itself in fear — a fear which could eventually mean its dissolution.

This fear, deeply rooted and multicentric in origin, is aiming the fullness of its grip toward our women and children. It is amply manifest, day in and day out, by the members of today's so-termed "affluent society" in their unwillingness to give of themselves to others. For some strange reason (one which is shortchanging more and more people as time passes), we have become, in a very striking way, a society in which one's own personal self takes total precedence over the selves of others. We have reached a state of self-orientation while ignoring — and sometimes eliminating — the other.

As in the case of any new mode of behavior, rationalizations are being devised for our actions. Like the Negro slavery of the nineteenth century and the Black discrimination of the twentieth, we are collectively crying "unwanted!" — and again, it finds its base in the "less than human"...rationale. ...

When Garrett Hardin, Professor of Biology at the University of California, Santa Barbara, and one of the leading proponents of abortion, declares, in an article entitled "We Need Abortion for the Children's Sake," that to rid society of "unwanted" children "we must more and more emphasize the *non-right*" (emphasis his) "of the individual woman to continue a pregnancy in utter disregard of the interests of the significant persons in her life" (her husband, parents or friends?), and that, to achieve this, "we might emphasize the social sin of a girl's becoming pregnant without considering the interests of everyone else concerned," isn't he really advocating the abandonment of women? And when Keith B. Russell, M.D., past president of the American College of Obstetrics and Gynecology and also a leading pro-abortionist, refers to pregnancy as a "complication" of "sexuality," isn't he really abandoning both the women and the chidren?...

22

A PSYCHOLOGICAL PRICE

I think every woman — whatever her age, her background, or sexuality — has a trauma at destroying a pregnancy. A level of humanness is touched. This is a part of her own life. She destroys a pregnancy, she is destroying herself. There is no way it can be innocuous. One is dealing with the life force. It is totally beside the point whether or not you think a life is there. You cannot deny that something is being created and that this creation is physically happening.

Often the trauma may sink into the unconscious and never surface in the woman's lifetime. But it is not as harmless and casual an event as many in the pro-abortion crowd insist. A psychological price is paid, I can't say exactly what. It may be alienation, it may be a pushing away from human warmth, perhaps a hardening of the maternal instinct. Something happens on the deeper levels of a woman's consciousness when she destroys a pregnancy. I know that as a psychiatrist.

Dr. Julius Fogel of Columbia Hospital For Women in Washington, D.C., **Washington Post**, February 28, 1971.

The faithless abandonment of women and children, which is so overtly promoted in today's society, is rapidly becoming a part of "Americana." People unthinkingly promote and advocate it as much as they were all for Mom and apple pie in times past. Even the women themselves have undertaken this battle for abandonment, and all under the guise of "liberation"! What will eventually come from this growing irresponsibility is the awareness that it only expands and deepens the abortion of peoples. What gradually begins with the violent abortion of the unborn child, before long becomes de facto "social abortion." Women who seek abortion of their "unwanted child" find themselves "socially aborted" themselves, long before they seek the medical abortionist. They are aborted, rejected and unwanted by those close to them — their husbands, parents and friends. ...By the time these same women reach the abortionist (who at least identifies himself) they are already isolated and afraid; they feel literally trapped.

23

"Human Garbage" — This was the result of one morning's work in a Canadian teaching hospital. These babies had attained a fetal age of from 18-24 weeks before being killed by abortion."

And this is not all. The woman involved begins to reject and destroy herself — "self-abortion." Instead of accepting herself and the responsibility she has for her helpless child, she turns away from the reality of life and the expectation that she, too, can play a role in the ultimate direction in which she moves. She fails to recognize that she is at least partially independent of her circumstances and begins to close herself off from the constructive solutions to her dilemma and the opportunity for human dignity. A woman must value herself before she can value her child, and society must value women before they can value their unborn children.

The medical-technical abortion is one problem in the abortion controversy, the problem of absolute destruction of new life; but the rejection of a woman by those close to her ("social abortion") and the refusal of a woman to enter into her life situation ("self abortion") are ever-expanding, new problems which compose the eventual substance of societal break. "Social abortion" represents a not so subtle prelude to the "unwanted child" prejudice, while the woman's "self-abortion" represents her own unique decision to destroy.

How do we abolish the aborting society — one which turns its back on those who need assistance and incites people to turn their backs on themselves and their own lives? Certainly, the hearts of men must change! Man must open himself up to those around him — the people of his everyday existence. He must also open himself up from within. He must not be afraid to help, to be helped, or to help himself. Indeed, he must once again be reawakened to that joy which is inherent in giving. A certain lack of joy is substantive to the whole abortion problem, and a reawakening to this joy is essential if we are to ever again open ourselves to new life.

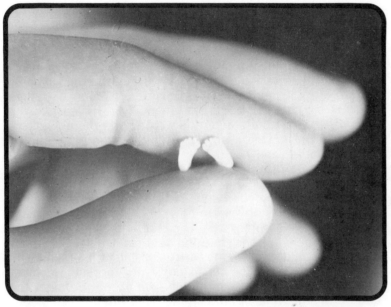

"Tiny Feet" — Tiny human feet at ten weeks, perfectly formed."

In order to begin our own participation in this change of heart, we must begin by recognizing that we are all, in one way or another, part of the aborting society (how many people have you rejected or been destructive to today?) Not until we as individuals begin to recognize our own participation in the aborting society — that we, everyday, close ourselves off from people around us and from ourselves; that we are, indeed, part of the problem — will we ever be able to become part of the solution. Our recognition of our participation in the aborting society must be on a deeply personal level; so personal, that it compels major attitudinal changes in our own self-extension.

25

Certainly, our society cannot accept the "unwanted prejudice," nor can it justly allow the mass slaughter of the unborn. What we can, and must, do is change our hearts, open our hands, extend our help and begin to deeply care. This is really the basis of an active love — an involvement in life, its beauties and its difficulties. This is the very best we have to offer the woman pregnant and distressed. And this is the only thing that will abolish the aborting society. ...

CONCLUSION

It has been said that if one is honestly in opposition to abortion, he then must be willing to extend his hand to those who need his help. If this is true, and we think that it is, then the extension of this statement is even more true; it is even more meaningful. If you allow yourself to become sensitized to the most diminutive of human beings, the unborn child, then you must also allow that sensitization to work deeply within you. You must allow it to sensitize you to all of human life: the old and the senile, the mentally retarded and the physically unrehabilitatable, the wanted and the unwanted, the white, black, yellow and red, the theist and the atheist, and the woman and her family who find a particular pregnancy distressful.

The paradox of modern man is his assumption that he can turn on and turn off, seemingly at will, the respect for human life. He assumes that he can offer a woman the very best while denying her child the very least. These assumptions are invalid because they are inconsistent. Human life is a continuum; and to be consistent in its respect, we must value the whole of this continuum. We cannot promote the quality of life while arbitrarily denying any aspect of our common humanity. We cannot kill a child and then say that this is the best we have to offer the mother.

The time has come for some real self-examination of ourselves as a people. We have been endowed with tremendous gifts and we possess enormous power; whether we use these gifts for good or for evil now depends on us. Will we passively submit to man's inhumanity to man, or will we silence the abortion cry with love and concern for our suffering neighbor?

THE ESSENCE: BALANCING RIGHTS

Daniel Callahan

Daniel Callahan, a Catholic lay theologian, is currently the director of the Institute of Society, Ethics and the Life Sciences, founded in 1969 to investigate the ethical impact of the biological revolution. He was formerly the executive editor of **The Commonweal Magazine**. His books include **The Mind of the Catholic Layman**, **Honesty In the Church**, **The New Church** and an important work on abortion, **Abortion: Law, Choice and Morality**, published in 1970. He is also the father of six children.

As you read consider the following questions:

1. Why is Mr. Callahan in favor of abortion on request?
2. What does he feel is the essence of the moral problem in the abortion debate?
3. What does Mr. Callahan feel is the "right way to experience abortion?"

Daniel Callahan, "Thinking and Experiencing," **Christianity and Crisis**, January 8, 1973, pp. 296-98. Reprinted from the January 8, 1973 issue of **Christianity and Crisis**, Copyright © 1973 by Christianity and Crisis, Inc.

A List of "minor" Truths

1. Permissive abortion laws do not encourage a greater or better use of contraceptives; on the contrary, such laws hinder that development.

2. There is no evidence yet from any country that, with enough time and availability of effective contraceptives, the number of abortions declines.

3. There is not yet a shred of evidence (good or bad) to show a direct, or even indirect, relationship between being an "unwanted child" and becoming a "battered child." Instead, present research is focussed more promisingly on quite a different set of variables (e.g., parents of battered children come from families in which they were battered children).

4. The woman most commonly seeking an abortion under permissive laws will not be the overburdened mother of many children (with that drunken husband, epileptic son and congenital syphillis), but an unmarried, very young woman of modest or relatively affluent means whose main "indication" for abortion will be her expressed wish not to have a (this) child (now).

5. The reason for the New York State Legislature's 1972 vote to repeal that state's present liberal abortion law (which was vetoed by Governor Rockefeller) was only in part the result of effective lobbying on the part of Right to Life groups. No less important was the local appearance of a worldwide phenomenon that I will call the "large number recoil syndrome"; that is, there will be a general public recoil from permissive laws when their net effect is to produce legal abortions that run into the hundreds of thousands (cf. Japan, Rumania, Bulgaria, Israel). Operative here seems to be the perception that, though abortion laws are liberalized primarily to deal with what are thought to be comparatively uncommon, highly-troubled pregnancies, resort to abortion quickly becomes routinized, serving as a primary (and repeated) method of birth control for many women, troubled or not.

6. Male legislators put restrictive abortion laws on the books (because they put all laws on the books). But it is no less true that where those laws have been removed or changed it has been male legislators who have done so

(Japan, Russia, Czechoslovakia, Great Britain, East Germany, India, California, New York). This fact is consistent with public opinion surveys that show that males are now, and have been for some decades, more favorable to liberalized abortion laws than women. And what is surprising about that? Is it not males who are still expected to bear the primary economic support of children and males who can panic as much as their wives or girl friends at the prospect of an unwanted child?

The sum total of all these "minor" truths is not to my mind great enough to overcome all the weightier reasons why abortion-on-request should be available to all women, old or young, married or unmarried, during the early months of pregnancy. My reasons for saying that are the familiar ones and do not need rehearsing in detail: the unwillingness and inability of the police to enforce rigid anti-abortion laws, the right of women to have control over their procreation, the serious and unresolvable problem of when human life should receive the full protection of the law (a situation requiring, I think, that the benefit of doubt be given to women and not fetuses).

The Essence: Balancing Rights

The essence of the moral problem in abortion is the proper way in which to balance the rights of the unborn (who very early have heads, fingers, toes, receptivity to stimuli, recordable EEG's and, from the start, have a unique, independent and ineluctably forward-moving genetic constitution — no less than you and me) against the right of a woman not to have a child she does not want. I am willing — no, well prepared — to grant her that right under law. I only ask that the society that grants this right be prepared to look with unblinking eyes at just what it is doing, not deceiving itself for one moment about even one aspect of what a granting of that right does.

The first result of having this right is, in practice, to nullify any and every social right one might be prepared in high ethical theory to grant to the unborn. Under permissive laws, any talk whatever of the "sanctity of life" of the unborn becomes a legal fiction. By giving women the full and total right to determine whether such a sanctity exists, the fetus is, in fact, given no legal or socially established standing whatever. I have always sought a method of having it both ways, with the law somehow granting women full freedom of choice while at the same time affording respect and protection to fetuses. The law does not allow such pious doublethink (though I will continue to entertain the idea); it forces a nasty either-or choice, devoid of a saving ethical ambiguity.

A second result is to force those who have fought for abortion-on-request to purge themselves systematically of doubts and reservation, and to find ways (revision of language, "counseling" designed to lull, evade and legitimate) of leading others to do likewise. This occurs for two reasons: (1) their opponents drive them to it by the accusatory extremeness of their hostility to abortion (usually combined with a glaring insensitivity to other important moral issues); and (2) they are themselves driven to it psychologically by the acutely impossible burden of any attempt to recognize both women and the unborn and to do justice to both. Something has to give, and it is usually earlier scruples and sensitivities about the unborn.

The third result is, in the best **1984** tradition, a reconstruction of history. This is done by creating a highly-charged mythology of male repression, or religious persecution, or puritanical fanaticism (i.e., whichever cue serves best at the moment to induce popular frenzy). By turning the "unwanted child" into the great known blight, history is further reconstructed into a Manichaen struggle between the wanted child (who can do no ill) and the unwanted child (who can do nothing but); and, not incidentally, values are reconstructed by making the value of a potential human being dependent upon being wanted by its mother. My own reading of history would ask only (a footnote will do) that mention be made of the women coerced into abortions by males, the one or two unwanted in the history of humankind who lived happy lives — that sort of thing.

What, then, is the right way to experience abortion? An answer to that question can be delayed no longer. For legislative purposes it should be experienced for what it is — an often necessary choice that women should be able to make for themselves without legal interference, even at the price of fetal rights. For purposes of a minimal sense of biological reality, it should also be experienced for what it is: the violent killing by dismemberment or deprivation of oxygen of one who, but for the wholly chance event that it happened to be unwanted, would otherwise have joined the rest of us who now walk, think, live and breathe — those we call human beings. For moral purposes it should also be recognized for what it is: a choice that, in the best of all

A WOMAN'S CONSCIENCE MUST BE GIVEN PRIORITY

Theology today allows to humankind far more control over nature and life than older theology permitted. Mountains can be moved not only by God through faith, but also by humans unleashing the power hidden in the atom. Scientists are developing the means of reproducing life by cloning from existing non-genital human cells. Society experiences population pressures unknown in previous times, pressures which demand restraint at least until such time as science and changing economics can adequately feed and support all lives. A theology for today must recognize the equal dignity of woman, controlling the fertility of her body, no longer captive to the male and the prodigality of nature. Clearly God has put into the hands of men and women powers of which earlier humankind could not dream. ...

There is true sanctity both in the unborn life of the womb and in the life of the living, breathing human being. It is God, the holy one, as Creator, Redeemer and Spirit who sanctifies them both. Each has a claim to value. The claim of the unborn life increases as it develops. When the claim to value of unborn life is seen to conflict with the claim of fully existent life, neither of these claims can be considered absolute. They must be weighed in the light of the total situation and of what would most conserve human and spiritual values.

The freedom of the individual conscience in the context of the human community must be affirmed. Where abortion is a possible decision, a woman's conscience must be given priority in the decision-making for only then can she live as being made in the image of God. At the same time women, as fully responsible beings and members of society, must place their decisions about abortion in the larger context of concern for life. In this context of conflicting values this participation in decision-making opens their lives to moral accountability. Thus no decision for abortion can responsibly be made lightly or carelessly.

From **Abortion: A Paper For Study** by a task force appointed by the National Council of Churches.

possible worlds, would never have to be made, but one that can be made in fear and trembling when it must be — with as much moral security as many another rotten decision imposed by a world most of us never made or chose.

The Right Way To Experience Abortion?

Finally, for social purposes, this recognition: the "must" that drives women to abortion is not one that need ineluctably to become individually more intensive and socially more extensive. Though abortion-on-request means the removal of all legally protectable fetal rights, it need not mean the end of all respect. That respect can be demonstrated in a number of ways.

Women could be given full freedom — not just freedom to have an abortion. This would include making it socially and economically possible for them to have those children they are presently deprived of by crass necessity. Respect could be shown if everything possible were done to see that abortion never becomes a routine decision, requiring instead always a hard, serious, probing self-examination, a self-examination incompatible with the language of "procedure" (which language assumes that, when all is said and done, women really are children, unable to face realities and take up the burden of adult moral choice). Finally, respect could be shown by more adequately publicizing the biological facts of pregnancy and gestation, which make it perfectly clear that the "product of conception" does bear a curious resemblance to a human being.

THE ABORTION CULTURE

Nick Thimmesch

Nick Thimmesch is a syndi-
cated columnist for the New
York newspaper **Newsday**.
He is based in Washington.

Use the following questions to assist your reading:

1. How does the author relate German medicine of the
   1930's to the abortion issue in our country today?
2. What dangers does Mr. Thimmesch see in some of the
   medical practices advocated in our country?
3. What is meant by the term ''the utilitarian ethic''? Why
   does the author feel that it is not as much a threat in the
   United States as it was in Nazi Germany?

Nick Thimmesch, ''The Abortion Culture,'' **Newsweek**, July 9, 1973, p. 7.
''Copyright Newsweek, Inc. 1973, reprinted by permission.''

Occasionally we come on to something that strikes the core and won't go away. For me, it has been the question of the value of human life — a question embracing abortion, letting the newborn die, euthanasia and the creeping utilitarian ethic in medicine that impinges on human dignity. It's all reminiscent of the "what is useful is good" philosophy of German medicine in the '30s — a utilitarianism that sent 275,000 "unworthy" Germans to death and helped bring on the Hitler slaughter of millions of human beings a few years later.

Now super-abortionists and others who relish monkeying around with human life cry that this is scare stuff inspired by hysterical Catholics waving picket signs. Not so. There is growing concern among Protestant and Jewish thinkers about "right to life" and the abortion-binge mentality.

Fetal life has become cheap. There were an estimated 1,340,000 legal and illegal abortions in the U.S. last year. There was a whopping 540,245 abortions in New York City in a 30-month period under the liberalized state abortion law. The abortion culture is upon us. In one operating room, surgeons labor to save a 21-week-old baby; in the next, surgeons destroy, by abortion, another child, who can also be reckoned to be 21 weeks old. Where is the healing?

PLASTIC BAGS

Look beyond the political arguments and see the fetus and what doctors do to it. An unborn baby's heartbeat begins between the 18th and 25th day; brain waves can be detected at seven weeks; at nine to ten weeks, the unborn squint, swallow and make a fist. Look at the marvelous photographs and see human life. Should these little human beings be killed unless it is to save the mother's life?

Other photos show this human life aborted, dropped onto surgical gauze or into plastic-bagged garbage pails. Take that human life by suction abortion and the body is torn apart, becoming a jumble of tiny arms and legs. In a D and C abortion, an instrument slices the body to pieces. Salt poisoning at nineteen weeks? The saline solution burns away the outer layer of the baby's skin. The ultimate is the hysterotomy (Caesarean section) abortion. As an operation, it can save mother and child; as an abortion it kills the child. Often, this baby fights for its life, breathes, moves and even cries. To see this, or the pictures of a plastic-bagged garbage can full of dead babies, well, it makes believers in right-to-life.

34

NURSES REACT TO ABORTIONS

Resigning her job in the delivery room of a hospital where she has assisted with abortions, the young nurse said she found "throwing away perfectly formed fetuses revolting."

"No matter what anyone tells you, and no matter what your religious beliefs," she said, "it's a physically grotesque thing to work at for eight hours a day." ...

"It's emotionally demanding and draining on all of us," explained a nurse who is planning on a family herself. "No matter how carefree, or disinterested or callous a woman is about her abortion, there comes a time in the procedure when she goes through some grave doubts. Maybe she's okay right up until the time the doctor injects the saline solution.

"Nurses are there to sustain her, to give her support as they would for any patient," she continued. "And it's difficult not to let her see our own nonverbal reactions. Very often she feels she is not doing the right thing and she looks to us as women for encouragement which we cannot give."

A registered nurse who had just left another hospital said: "I couldn't possibly go on ignoring the live fetuses; or even putting the dead ones in buckets to be sent to the lab. One day when I came on duty, the nurse going off duty pointed to the table on the other side of the room where the fetuses were placed. It was easy to detect from all the way across the room a visibly strong heart beat."

"The other nurse was timid and she asked me to speak to the doctor," the nurse continued. "When I pointed it out to him he said, 'For all intents and purposes, it's dead. Leave it there.' I told him I couldn't do it. He could have my job on the line, but I wouldn't do it. This time I was going to bring it to the nursery. I knew the fetus would probably die, but I had to give it a chance. I had to treat it as a human being."

In most hospitals each fetus, depending on size, is placed in either an individual carton or buckets containing a formalin solution, and then sent to the lab for pathological examination. Most labs do not remain open on the weekends. According to one nurse, "you could populate a whole village with the fetuses in cartons lined up on the table on Monday morning."

The nurses who resent abortions usually don't hold it against the doctors.

"In the hospital I used to work in, only 10 per cent of the doctors would do abortions and then only on their own patients or the daughters of the patients," one nurse said. "It was these young girls, the daughters of the older patients, that I really felt sorry for.

"They were usually scared, and many didn't want an abortion on moral grounds. But they were forced by their mothers. And abortion for them is not a solution. What they need is more and better sex education."

Doris Revere Peters, **N.Y. Nurses Quit Over Abortions**, reprinted with permission from NC News Service, Washington, D.C. 20005.

It's unfair to write this way, cry the super-abortionists, or to show the horrible photos. But Buchenwald and Dachau looked terrible, too. Abortions are always grisly tragedies. This truth must be restated at a time when medical administrators chatter about "cost-benefit analysis" factors in deciding who lives and who dies.

THE 'GOOD DEATH'

The utilitarian ethic is also common in the arguments of euthanasia advocates at work in six state legislatures. Their euphemisms drip like honey (should I say, cyanide?) just as they did in Germany — "death with dignity," the "good death." Their legal arguments fog the mind. Their mentality shakes me. One doctor, discussing the suicide-prone, wrote: "In such instances, positive euthanasia — a nice, smooth anesthetic to terminate life — appears preferable to suicide." Dr. Russell Sackett, author of the "Death With Dignity" bill in Florida, said: "Florida has 1,500 mentally retarded and mentally ill patients, 90 per cent of whom should be allowed to die." The German utilitarians had concluded the same when they led the first group of mental patients to the gas chamber at the Sonnestein Psychiatric Hospital in 1939. It bothers me that eugenicists in Germany organized the mass destruction of mental patients, and in the United States pro-abortionists now also serve in pro-euthanasia organizations. Sorry, but I see a pattern.

Utilitarianism isn't all abortion or euthanasia. Utilitarians ran the experiment in which syphilitic black men died through lack of penicillin. There are also experiments on free-clinic patients, students, the institutionalized. Senate hearings revealed that two experimental birth-control drugs were used on the "vulnerable" for purposes other than those approved by the Food and Drug Administration.

This monkeying around with people is relentless. Some medics would like to sterilize institutionalized people from here to breakfast. Psychosurgery is performed on hundreds of Americans annually, not to correct organic brain damage, but to alter their behavior. This chancy procedure, a first cousin of the now discredited prefrontal lobotomy that turned 50,000 Americans into human vegetables, is performed on unruly children and violence-prone prisoners.

Experimenters produce life outside the womb — combining sperm and ovum — and dispose of the human zygotes by pouring the solution down the sink drain. Recently scientists debated guidelines for experimenting with the live human fetus. To those considering the fetus as an organ, like, say, a kidney, Dr. Andre Hellegers of Georgetown University pointed out that fetuses have their own organs and cannot be considered organs themselves. How does one get consent from a live fetus? he asked. Or even from its donors — the parents who authorized the abortion?

Once fetal experimentation is sanctioned, are children to be next? Farfetched? No. In the New England Journal of Medicine, Dr. Franz Ingelfinger recently advocated removing the World Medical Association's absolute ban on experimenting with children and mental incompetents.

We can brake the tendencies of technocratic-minded doctors and administrators coldly concerned with "cost-benefit analysis." There was no such brake in Germany. After the first killings at Sonnestein, respected German doctors, not Nazi officials, killed 275,000 patients in the name of euthanasia. Many were curable. Eventually the doomed "undesirables" included epileptics, mental defectives, World War I amputees, children with "badly modeled ears" and "bed wetters."

UTILITARIAN ETHIC

The worst barbarisms often have small beginnings. The logical extension of this utilitarian ethic was the mass exterminations in slave-labor camps. In "A Sign for Cain," Dr. Frederic Wertham tells how death-dealing technicians from German state hospitals (and their equipment) were moved to the camps in 1942 to begin the big job.

Could the "what is useful is good" mentality lead to such horror in the U.S.? Not so long as I am allowed to write like this — which German journalists couldn't. Not so long as right-to-life Americans can dispute — which Germans couldn't. The extremes of the utilitarian mentality rampaging today through medicine, the drug industry and government will be checked by our press, lawmakers and doctors, lawyers and clergymen holding to the traditional ethic . The Germans weren't blessed that way.

DISTINGUISHING BETWEEN FACT AND OPINION

This discussion exercise is designed to promote experimentation with one's ability to distinguish between fact and opinion. It is a fact, for example, that the United States was militarily involved in the Vietnam War. But to say this involvement served the interests of world peace is an opinion or conclusion. Future historians will agree that American soldiers fought in Vietnam, but their interpretations about the causes and consequences of the war will probably vary greatly.

Part I

Instructions

Most of the following statements are taken from the readings in this book; some have other origins. Consider each statement carefully. Mark (O) for any statement you feel is an opinion or interpretation of the facts. Mark (F) for any statement you believe is a fact. Discuss and compare your judgments with those of other class members.

> O = Opinion
> F = Fact

_____ 1. Abortion violates the God-given natural law.

_____ 2. The movement for abortion on demand is a symptom of a selfish society.

_____ 3. Abortion is an effective method of limiting population.

_____ 4. The human fetus does not become a human person until after birth. -

_____ 5. The unborn fetus deserves the same care we give the retarded and other handicapped individuals in our society.

_____ 6. Abortions are more easily obtained by wealthy women.

_____ 7. The decision to abort is often the best choice one can make between available alternatives in an imperfect world.

_____ 8. Rape should be sufficient reason to abort, regardless of the age of the fetus.

_____ 9. Any state law that denies a pregnant woman an abortion during the first three months of her pregnancy is unconstitutional.

_____ 10. Abortion is the first step to the complete disregard for life that was characteristic of Nazi Germany.

_____ 11. Carrying an unwanted baby to term is less traumatic for the mother than the consequences of deliberate abortion.

_____ 12. In the U.S., abortions may be legally performed at any time before birth under certain circumstance.

_____ 13. Men, not women, in the Western world, have traditionally made the decision of whether or not to abort.

_____ 14. No woman should be forced to have a child she does not want.

Part II

Instructions

STEP 1. The class should break into groups of four to six students.

STEP 2. Each small group should try to locate two statements of fact and two statements of opinion in the book. First examine reading number six and then turn to other readings if necessary.

STEP 3. Each group should choose a student to record its statements.

EUTHANASIA

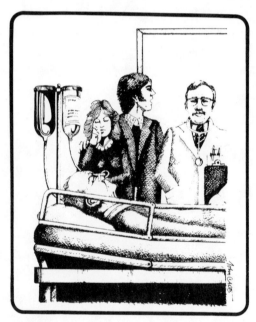

Readings

I FAVOR MERCY

Stewart V. Pahl

Stewart V. Pahl is a Humanist Counselor, a member of the American Humanist Association and of the National Writers Club. He has studied euthanasia, or "good death," since 1971 and has written several articles on the subject. He has also lectured on the topic in Florida, New York, Illinois and Washington, D.C.

Consider the following questions while reading:

1. What does the author mean by the statement "I favor mercy"?
2. What safeguards does the author recommend to insure that the practice of euthanasia is not abused?
3. How does he react to the possibility that the practice of euthanasia will be abused and used improperly?

Stewart V. Pahl, "I Favor Mercy," **The Humanist**, September/October, 1972, pp. 37-38. This article first appeared in **The Humanist**, September/October, 1972 and is reprinted by permission.

Everyone terminates life prematurely. Even vegetarians terminate the lives of plants, and step on a worm occasionally. When we discuss this issue, the major considerations, therefore, have to do with degree, manner, and intent; there is no question as to "whether," since we all terminate life for other entities. The main questions are: much or little, cruel or merciful, intentional or unintentional.

Nature itself terminates most lives long before their longevity expectancy. Millions of sperm die for each one that lives. Further, the number of human lives terminated by "natural causes" far exceeds the number of those ending when a person simply does not awaken some morning after he has reached the age of 100 or 120.

I favor merciful termination of life; no discussion necessary. I favor intentional termination of life, since most of us engage in such action without giving it much thought. I favor owning one's own life.

Some time ago, it was almost unheard of that a person could own his own body. Next of kin owned the body after death. Now, in many states, a person can will his body to a medical school, for example, and such a pre-death statement of intent is binding upon next of kin. Some day, the law will shift so that individuals will own their own lives as well as their own bodies.

Obviously, this will make suicide legal. I regret this somewhat, but not to the point of being greatly disturbed. The greater good derives from the possibility of legalizing euthanasia for those who want it. Safeguarded euthanasia would eliminate most of the necessity of caring for "vegetables," a necessity that now preempts manpower that should be devoted to the living, not to the dying and the already "dead." It would eliminate much unnecessary suffering; it would make a satisfying departure possible in many instances where a degrading, repulsive death is now the only legal possibility.

It would be easy to include safeguards, so that a few euthanasianists could not arbitrarily do away with all rich kinfolk for the sake of money-hungry inheritors. Reasonable precautions might include such provisions as these:
1. The state could stipulate the number of individuals who should agree when euthanasia might be practiced. This could be, for example, three persons: two M.D.'s and one nearest of kin.

2. The state could stipulate how frequently an individual, or group of individuals, may be permitted to sign a euthanasia authorization. The rule might be: ''No two persons shall sign a euthanasia authorization oftener than twice a year.'' This safeguard would prevent two or three ''professional euthanasianists'' from habitually signing authorizations — for a fee, of course, depending upon how much the beneficiaries were to inherit.

3. The state might well stipulate that no euthanasia could be authorized except when so directed by the individual himself (generally on a prior basis, when in good health and sound mind). Rare exceptions would be made in some cases, when a person had for some time been legally incompetent and medically incurable.

A NEW ETHIC IS EMERGING

The traditional Western ethic has always placed great emphasis on the intrinsic worth and equal value of every human life regardless of its stage or condition. ... This traditional ethic is still clearly dominant, but there is much to suggest that it is being eroded at its core and may eventually even be abandoned. ...

It seems safe to predict that the new demographic, ecological and social realities and aspirations are so powerful that the new ethic of relative rather than of absolute and equal values will ultimately prevail as man exercises ever more certain and effective control over his numbers, and uses his always comparatively scarce resources to provide the nutrition, housing economic support, education and health care in such ways as to achieve his desired quality of life and living.

Editorial in **California Medicine**, September, 1970, pp. 67-68.

It will be said that there will be abuses; this is true. I know of no custom, however good, that does not have its abuses. It is said that practicing some euthanasia will make it progressively acceptable to do away with everybody who becomes a slight nuisance to anybody else. This is absurd. The state has engaged in legalized termination of life for many centuries, and never yet has this practice become so out of hand as to deplete the population beyond recovery. When abuses increase unbearably, the people revise the statutes. No laws or customs are perfect.

For our own time, and for a generation or two, I think it would be on the side of decency and mercy to permit (the law doesn't have to do more than permit) limited, safeguarded euthanasia. No amount of sentimentalizing can hide the fact that hundreds, even thousands, of elderly persons would cheerfully kiss the world farewell if only they were permitted to do this legally and gracefully. Among the living, some would applaud this decision selfishly and some would applaud unselfishly.

Traditionally, we have been both sentimental and cruel in dealing with human lives. We've been sentimental when a child has fallen into a well, for example, and we have commanded incalculable manpower and material to rescue the child. But if someone had suggested previously that we spend $3.27 in order to cover the abandoned well satisfactorily so that a child couldn't fall into it, we would have turned away and shrugged, cruelly, indifferently. In general, that's the way we have too often dealt with life and death.

In early American days, as now, no physician would have dared to practice euthanasia. Yet the sentimental state that forbade this merciful custom of euthanasia was the selfsame cruel state that legalized slavery. We have a long inherited history of cruelty and sentimentality flourishing side by side in our customs, our laws, our attitudes.

I propose mercy. I place human wellbeing at the top of my list of priorities. I am willing to redefine "life" and "death" for the sake of such human well-being. When "life" is gone, let us govern ourselves accordingly and be decent toward the "remains."

46

EUTHANASIA AND
THE NEW ETHIC

John M. Hendrickson & Thomas St. Martin

Thomas St. Martin is a past president of Minnesota Citizens Concerned for Life and presently holds an administrative position in the Minnesota Department of Education.
John M. Hendrickson is a radiologist in St. Paul, Minnesota. He lectures on the topic of Euthanasia in the Minnesota area and is a member of the board of directors of Minnesota Citizens Concerned for Life.

Use the following questions to assist you in your reading:

1. What is meant by the term **new ethic**?
2. What do the authors claim is the basic fallacy of the euthanasia argument?
3. What is the distinction between **positive** euthanasia and **negative** euthanasia?

John M. Hendrickson and Thomas St. Martin, ''Euthanasia and the 'New Ethic','' **The Wanderer**, August 16, 1973. Reprinted with permission from **The Wanderer**.

47

We have been propelled into the abortion era by a new ethic which places relative value on human life; the same ethic has now brought us to the threshold of the euthanasia era. The notion that each and every human life (regardless of condition or social "usefulness") is inviolable has been eroded. It is being rapidly replaced by a philosophy of over-practical realism — by a philosophy which understands "rightness" and "goodness" in terms of "usefulness." Life is no longer an absolute "good" in and of itself; the taking of life is justified in the interests of ensuring the greatest good for the greatest number. Thus, the relatively "useless" lives of the pre-natal human being or the aged human being can be destroyed in the interests of some greater social "benefit." In effect, the new ethic tells us that certain kinds of people in certain circumstances, are worth more dead than alive.

The basic fallacy of the euthanasia argument is this belief that life is expendable (under certain conditions), and worse, that some men are able to discern when another man's life falls into that category. It is the result of a falsification of life that our Madison Avenue society has created; that unless we are youthful, beautiful, intelligent and physically whole our lives cannot be fully worthwhile or "useful." We must reject this vicious doctrine and realize that the gift of life itself is the basis for everything else.

But what is euthanasia? Strictly defined, it means "good death." According to the dictionary it means "...inducing the painless death of a person for reasons assumed to be merciful." A common synonym is "mercy killing."

Anyone who has seen a close relative or friend dying from a hopelessly incurable and unbearably painful illness (such as terminal cancer) feels the weight of the argument that the "humane" thing to do is to painlessly help the suffering patient out of his misery. Herein lies the superficial appeal of the pro-euthanasia argument.

This does not mean that a hopelessly ill patient must be kept alive by any and every means available. Everyone accepts the principle that the use of extraordinary means is not required in every case.

Our real concern must be with what is often termed "positive" euthanasia (as distinct from "negative" euthanasia — the withholding of life sustaining measures from a hopelessly ill or dying patient). The concept of positive euthanasia centers on the distinction between causing death to occur and permitting death to occur; a distinction between active and passive behavior.

To actively terminate a human life for whatever motives (whether "mercy" or social "benefit") is a philosophy that the medical profession, as preservers of life, must never embrace and which a democratic and humanitarian society must never accept. It would involve climbing onto a greased slide from which no one can escape. If we can end the life of a hopeless cancer patient, then what is to stop us from acting similarly with the patient with hopeless brain damage or the senility of old age? What is to stop us from including the hopelessly mentally ill or retarded, or the bedridden who have become a burden to themselves and others? What of the incompetent patient who cannot give permission to terminate his life; who can decide his life is not worth living?

These superficially appealing euthanasia arguments have frightening corollaries and if they are accepted all our lives are in danger.

DEATH WITH DIGNITY?

Current arguments for euthanasia — literally, "good death" — often make use of the phrase "death with dignity." The assumption here is that pain so intense as to be "unendurable" degrades the sufferer, robs him of his dignity. This in turn implies that we know what constitutes the dignity of the sufferer. But dignity is a very imprecise concept, and in any case is not a Christian concept, though it may be consonant with Christian views. ...

The contemporary stress on euthanasia can be seen in part as evidence of our culture's pervasive concern for what is cosmetically pleasing. [The same holds for present-day ecological awareness.] With this concern goes the belief [usually unstated] that pain — physical suffering, in this instance — is life's greatest evil. Physical suffering — what about psychic suffering? So far as I have been able to discover, not a single proponent of passive euthanasia for the "hopelessly ill" has ever argued on behalf of euthanasia for the "hopelessly insane." Yet insanity or mental illness is very often a form of suffering, of psychic, as contrasted to physical, pain. Moreover, insanity is "undignified" and cosmetically displeasing. Perhaps that is why our society's treatment of the "mentally ill" remains scandalous. We seem to think of pain as physical suffering, which must be overcome at (nearly) any cost for the sake of "dignity."

Now, as I said above, I consider the idea of dignity basically abstract and not particularly Christian. First, it is abstract because it operates on the assumption that we know what is a fitting, a worthy death for a human being, and because it ignores the specificity of the person and deals with him as one human instance under the generalizing concept of "dignity." More fundamental, especially for the Christian, is my second point. We do not yet fully know what it is to be human; and because we do not know, we cannot, or ought not, glibly speak of "human dignity."

Robert M. Cooper, "Euthanasia and The Notion of 'Death with Dignity, ' " **Christian Century**, February 21, 1973, p. 225. Dr. Cooper is Assistant Professor of Ethics and Moral Theology at Nashotah House (Episcopal), Nashotah, Wisconsin. Copyright 1973 Christian Century Foundation. Reprinted by permission from the February 21, 1973 issue of the **Christian Century**.

MY VIEWS ON EUTHANASIA

Margaret Mead

Dr. Mead is one of the foremost anthropologists in the country. Her expeditions to New Guinea and Bali during a period of over thirty years have resulted in many books and numerous journal and magazine articles. In addition to many other honors and accomplishments, she is a teacher and a past president of the American Anthropology Association, and currently maintains an office at the American Museum of Natural History in New York City.

The following questions will help you to examine the reading:

1. What right should an incurably ill person have in the opinion of Dr. Mead?
2. What role should the doctor play in euthanasia decisions?

Margaret Mead, ''Margaret Mead Answers,'' **Redbook**, July, 1973, pp. 33-34. Reprinted from **Redbook Magazine**, July, 1973, Copyright © 1973 The McCall Publishing Company. (UPI photo)

I do not believe that a society should have the power to decide that old people are useless or dispensable or no longer capable of living humanly and so end their lives. A society as such should not have this kind of power over human life, whether it is the old or the unborn, the feeble-minded or the desperately handicapped, whose lives are involved. It is our responsibility, especially in a society as rich as ours, to care for those who are in need of care.

It is true that among primitive peoples living on the edge of extinction — a small band of food gatherers in a period of extreme drought, for example — it may sometimes be necessary to decide who is to survive. But even in such cases we find that most societies try to save old people as long as they can or, as among the Eskimos, let them choose when it seems best to die.

I do believe that a person who is very old or incurably ill should have that choice. But this also presents problems. At the point at which an old person no longer is able to relate in any way to his relatives and friends, he is not able to make the necessary decision. It now is advocated that the oxygen machine should be turned off when the brain is dead, even if the heart beats on; but someone must make the decision to turn off the machine.

Clearly the choice must be made long before the crisis occurs. And just as it is customary for people to make their last will and testament when they are well, in order to avoid the pressures and the forced or erratic decisions of a death-bed will, so also it is possible for persons to decide in advance and put in writing — as with a will — the circumstances under which they would want medical intervention and under what circumstances they would wish to have no further intervention.

I myself would wish to live as long as I could be a thinking and communicating person; I would not want to live as an uncommunicating body. As physicians generally respect the whose convenience is euthanasia really intended? they also would be able to respect, with a clear conscience, the wishes their patients have set down earlier. And families would not be guiltridden about decisions made long before.

A further difficulty arises for the old person who does not need special medical intervention merely to keep him or her alive but who faces inevitable deterioration, pain and personality distortion. There is at present a group advocating

52

legislation to permit a physician to give a pill, at the request of the patient, that would give release from the suffering ahead. I believe it is the right of an individual to choose not to endure destructive suffering that can end only in death.

THE LIVING WILL

TO MY FAMILY, MY PHYSICIAN, MY CLERGYMAN, MY LAWYER —

If the time comes when I can no longer take part in decisions for my own future, let this statement stand as the testament of my wishes:

If there is no reasonable expectation of my recovery from physical or mental disability,

I, _____
request that I be allowed to die and not be kept alive by artificial means or heroic measures. Death is as much a reality as birth, growth, maturity and old age — it is the one certainty. I do not fear death as much as I fear the indignity of deterioration, dependence and hopeless pain. I ask that medication be mercifully administered to me for terminal suffering even if it hastens the moment of death.

This request is made after careful consideration. Although this document is not legally binding, you who care for me will, I hope, feel morally bound to follow its mandate. I recognize that it places a heavy burden of responsibility upon you, and it is with the intention of sharing that responsibility and of mitigating any feelings of guilt that this statement is made.

Signed _____ Date _____

Witnessed by: _____

The Living Will, prepared by the Euthanasia Educational Council, directs the signer's family to avoid the use of extraordinary measures to maintain life in terminal illness.

But I also believe we should not put on practicing physicians the double burden of being honest with their patients — and their patients' families — in telling them what lies ahead and of assisting their patients to end their lives. In a great many early cultures the power to cure and the power to kill were lodged in the same person. It was a great step forward in the history of medicine when care and curing were separated from any other power, and I do not think we should do anything to jeopardize this dedication of the physician to the life and well-being of his individual patients.

The power of assisting the individual who elects to die with dignity should be vested in a board that is committed legally to respect the person's need and way of meeting it. Such a board would have to be made up of persons with medical training — for example, public-health officials — but not men and women engaged in the medical care of the individual.

I believe individuals should have the choice of euthanasia. But such a choice must be set within a framework of ethical commitment to the value of human life.

EVALUATING SOURCES

A critical thinker must always question his various sources of information. Historians, for example, usually distinguish between primary sources (eyewitness accounts) and secondary sources (writing based on primary or eye-witness accounts, or other secondary sources). Most text-books are examples of secondary sources. A diary written by a Civil War Veteran about his war experiences is one example of a primary source concerning the Civil War. In order to be a critical reader one must be able to recognize primary sources. However, this is not enough. Eyewitness accounts do not always provide accurate descriptions. Historians may find ten different eyewitness accounts of an event and all the accounts might interpret the event differently. Then they must decide which of these accounts provide the most objective and accurate interpretations.

Test your skill in evaluating by participating in the following exercise. Pretend you are living 2000 years in the future. Your teacher tells you to write an essay analyzing the events leading up to the Voluntary Family Limitation Act of 1984. (See page 57)

Consider carefully each of the following source descriptions.

FIRST, underline only those descriptions you feel would serve as a primary source for your essay.

SECOND, rank only the underlined or primary sources assigning the number (1) to the most objective and accurate primary source, number (2) to the next most accurate and so on until the ranking is finished. Then discuss and compare your evaluations with other class members.

Assume that all of the following essays, articles, books and speeches deal with the events leading up to the Voluntary Family Limitation Act of 1984.

1. An address to the nation by President John Highland who signed the bill, making it a law.

2. The Prime Minister of England, writing in 1984

3. A sociologist, writing in 1992

4. An historian, writing in 1987

5. A report by a presidential commission on population problems, issued in 1978

6. A U.S. senator's speech against the proposed legislation in 1983

7. A newspaper editorial supporting the act in 1984

8. A statement against the proposed legislation by the National Council of Churches in 1983

9. An article written by an African journalist in 1985

The Voluntary Family Limitation Act
Public Welfare Law No. 376251
Date of Promulgation — Jan. 1, 1984

Whereas, the freedom to procreate has become an intolerable burden for our citizens,

Whereas, surplus population is the basic cause of all our national ills and therefore a direct threat to the welfare of our nation,

Whereas, parenthood is a right extended to society and the individual by the state,

Whereas, large families violate the personal rights of their first born by breeding excess offspring which insure that all their children will have less and thereby be less, and,

Whereas, voluntary family limitation measures supported by unrestricted abortion and sterilization have failed to bring about the desired optimum population level.

The following provisions shall be effective immediately

1. All citizens, male and female, who have reached their 10th birthday shall report to their local public health clinic and be immunized with a reversible antifertility drug until such time when they shall choose to beget offspring.

2. Every couple shall be permitted to bear two natural children (this number shall be subject to change by the proper authorities in accordance with the socioeconomic needs of the state).

3. To insure compliance with the law at all levels of government, a National Voluntary Birth Limitation Cabinet shall be established at the federal level. In addition to its policing and investigating powers, the NVBLC shall establish appropriate guidelines and issue suitable child quotas to its regional, state and local boards.

4. Failure to comply with the law shall result in a fine and/or imprisonment of one or both parents. Showing themselves to be unfit parents by their total disregard for the quality of life of society, such persons shall relinquish all rights to their surplus children who, in turn, are to be placed for adoption or institutionalized by the state.

James J. Diamond, M.D. and Randy Engel, **Suicide: American Style**. A Liguorian pamphlet by the Redemptorist Fathers.

THE AMERICAN WAY OF DEATH

M. Stanton Evans

M. Stanton Evans is the editor of **The Indianapolis News**. He is a former assistant editor of **The Freeman** and managing editor of **Human Events Newsletter**, and is currently an associate editor and regular columnist for **The National Review**. His books include **The Liberal Establishment**, **Revolt on the Campus**, **The Politics of Surrender**, **The Lawbreakers**, and **The Future of Conservatism**.

Bring the following questions to your reading:

1. For whose convenience is euthanasia really intended?
2. Why does the author feel that euthanasia represents a reversal of some of the basic values of our civilization?
3. What future dangers does the author foresee if euthanasia becomes an everyday occurrence in our society?

M. Stanton Evans, ''The American Way of Death,'' **Human Events**, September 1, 1973. Reprinted with permission from **Human Events**.

When the campaign to promote permissive abortion was commenced in earnest a few years back, opponents warned that this was only the beginning and that mercy-killing of the old and ailing would follow in its turn.

Such warnings were brushed aside or ignored in the abortion debate, treated as alarmist propaganda. Abortion, after all, concerned the right of a woman to her own body, and disposing of the "products of conception" was no more a matter of civic concern than clipping one's finger-nails or having a tooth pulled — at least according to the proponents. The notion that life itself was at stake in the struggle, argued by the critics, was casually dismissed from consideration by abortion proponents, including the U.S. Supreme Court.

Now it develops the critics of abortion have been right all along — that the killing of the child in embryo is but the beginning of a massive assault on life.

The "new ethic" suggested by the easy acceptance of abortion is seeking conquests beyond the womb, beginning with the aged and infirm. No sooner had the Supreme Court's abortion decision taken hold, indeed; than we were subjected to a drumfire of publicity about the "right to die," the advantage of mercy-killing, and the subtle joys of "death with dignity." The predicted drive for euthanasia is spreading across America, exactly according to schedule.

Thus we are treated to media puffery, including TV entertainments, about the undignified state of people kept alive by expensive hospital machinery, clearly suggesting the superior attractiveness of death. A nationally distributed news feature describes the outlook of an aged lady who "does not want to hang on, like too many of her friends, wired into tubes and respirators...in effect, a living mummy, a degradation of life, a defilement of death." This lady has executed a "living will" which urges her family, friends and physician to pull the plug and let her die if she reaches that condition.

Such notions are apparently spreading. The Euthanasia Society of America which promotes the "living will" idea and advocates "passive euthanasia," (letting people die instead of killing them outright) claims a quantum jump in membership over the past four years. The head of the organization reports the number of members has grown from 600 in 1969 to 50,000 today, and that the "living will" procedure is catching on. She asserts that "we had a bride and groom the other day who wanted to sign the 'living will' as part of their mutual understanding, which I thought was very sweet.''

Acceptance of euthanasia is confirmed by the Gallup Poll — which shows a startling rise in the percentage of the American population that looks with favor on the idea of mercy killing. In 1950 the affirmative responses on the question came to 36 per cent. This year the proportion is up to 53 per cent. The most notable rise in favorable answers has occurred among those under 30 years of age. Two decades ago the ''yes'' response to mercy killing was only 30 per cent; today it stands at an enormous 67 per cent. Among those with college educations, the ''yes'' response has gone from 34 per cent to 61.

As with abortion, the argument for mercy killing is being made by emotional exploitation of hard cases: Instances of terminal cancer patients stuck full of tubes, allegedly wanting to die but prevented from doing so by outmoded value systems.

DOCTORS IN NAZI GERMANY

Doctors in Nazi Germany started with the acceptance of that attitude, basic in the euthanasia movement, that there is such a thing as life not worthy to be lived. This attitude in its early stages concerned itself merely with the severely and chronically sick. Gradually the sphere of those to be included in this category was enlarged to include the socially unproductive, the racially unwanted, and finally all non-Germans. But it is important to realize that the infinitely small wedged-in lever from which this entire trend of mind received its impetus was the attitude toward the nonrehabilitable sick.

L. Anderson, **New England Journal of Medicine**, 241: 39-47.

With abortion it was victims of rape or incest — statistically insignificant factors in the widespread slaughter of the unborn which is now occurring in this country to suit the convenience of their parents. (Exactly how widespread may be inferred from the fact that in New York State last year there were more abortions than live births — by a margin of 278,600 to 252,278.)

On that analogy, it is logical to suspect the euthanasia drive embraces similar motives. Who is really being considered in the demand for mercy killings? The victims who will be permitted to die or actively dispatched, or the friends and relatives who find the old and infirm to be an emotional and financial nuisance? Dr. Milton Helpern, chief medical examiner of New York City, thinks it's the latter. He says he is opposed to euthanasia and observes that it's "done for the convenience of the family...It's the family that can't stand the suffering. A patient who's in a coma isn't in pain. It's the family who's in pain." Such pain is quenched most readily by letting the patient slip away.

The issue here is the fundamental attitude toward life expressed in both the euthanasia and abortion campaigns. Each suggests the life of human beings is a relative value to be weighed in the scales of social convenience and disposed of according to utilitarian considerations — with the weakest members of the species, unborn or aged or ill, the first to go. This represents a major reversal of Judaeo-Christian conceptions concerning the sacredness of life, and a movement back to ancient pagan notions which countenanced numerous rituals of death, including abortion and infanticide. (It is noteworthy in this connection that the Supreme Court ruling on abortion offers favorable reference to the pro-abortion stance of "ancient religion," in contrast to the historic positions of Judaism and Christianity.)

That the anti-life campaign implies a reversal of civilizational values at the deepest level is suggested by a remarkable editorial which appeared a few years back in the journal of the California Medical Association. This editorial states that the drive for abortion is in fact a rejection of the Judaeo-Christian social ethic at its very core — a direct assault on life itself. What is really being decided in the abortion debate, the editorial argues, is that some shall live while others die, and that it is up to physicians with their special expertise to assist in making these difficult choices.

"Since the old ethic has not yet been fully displaced," says the editorial, "it has been necessary to separate the idea of abortion from the idea of killing, which continues to be socially abhorrent. The result has been a curious avoidance of the scientific fact, which everyone really knows, that human life begins at conception and is continuous whether intra- or extra-uterine until death. ... It is suggested that this schizophrenic sort of subterfuge is necessary because while a new ethic is being accepted the old one has not yet been rejected."

The editorial stresses the repudiation of Western religious values implicit in this procedure, observing that problems of pollution and population growth confront us "with the necessity of deciding what is to be preserved and strengthened and what is not, and that this will of necessity violate the traditional Western ethic. ... It will become necessary to place relative rather than absolute values on such things as human lives, the usage of scarce resources, and the various elements which are to make up the quality of life or living which is to be sought. This is quite distinctly at variance with the Judaeo-Christian ethic. ..."

Indifference toward life is closely tied to conceptions of the all-powerful state which manipulated the destiny of its citizens and an elite which has the right and duty to make such awful choices.

Potential applications may be seen in recent suggestions for genetic engineering and the statement some months ago of the head of the National Academy of Science that the time may arrive when we shall have to weed out the genetically unfit by abortion. He explained that much of society now feels "the early fetus is a nonperson, an extension of the woman involved" and that "it is a question of whether the welfare of the species is more important than the welfare of the individual."

Exactly the same arguments can be brought to bear on the question of euthanasia on the principle that some lives are "better" or "more viable" than others — and somebody in the know will have to make the tough decision.

Consider the statement of Prof. Robert Morison of Cornell on the subject of stopping life-support systems for the critically ill: "Squirm as we may to avoid the inevitable, it seems time to admit to ourselves that there is simply no hiding place and that we must shoulder the responsibility of deciding in such a way as to hasten the declining trajectory of some lives, while doing our best to slow down the decline of others. And we have to do this on the basis of some judgment on the quality of the life in question."

The unborn, the old, the sickly and unfit — where, exactly, does the process stop? Every resident of the 20th Century with its gallery of totalitarian horrors can provide a ready answer to that question.

THE CASE FOR EUTHANASIA

Joseph Fletcher

Joseph Fletcher is the author of **Situation Ethics: The New Morality** and **Moral Responsibility: Situation Ethics at Work**. He is well known as a lecturer and author, both in the U.S. and abroad. He is currently Visiting Professor of Medical Ethics at the University of Virginia. Formerly he served as Dean of St. Paul's Cathedral, Cincinnati and Professor of Social Ethics, Episcopal Theology School, Cambridge, Massachusetts.

Reflect on the following questions while you read:

1. Why does Dr. Fletcher feel that the horror of Nazi Germany's euthanasia practices do not apply to our country's discussion of euthanasia?
2. What does Dr. Fletcher mean when he says that "it is **personal** function that counts, not **biological** function?"
3. What four forms of euthanasia does the author describe?
4. What does the author feel is the highest good and how does it relate to euthanasia?

Joseph Fletcher, "Ethics and Euthanasia," **To Live and to Die: When, Why, and How**, ed. Robert H. Williams (New York: Springer-Verlag, 1973, pp. 113-22. Reprinted with permission from Springer-Verlag.

It is harder morally to justify letting somebody die a slow and ugly death, dehumanized, than it is to justify helping him to escape from such misery. This is the case at least in any code of ethics which is humanistic or personalistic, i.e., in any code of ethics which has a value system that puts humanness and personal integrity above biological life and function. It makes no difference whether such an ethics system is grounded in a theistic or a naturalistic philosophy. We may believe that God wills human happiness or that man's happiness is, as Protagoras thought, a self-validating standard of the good and the right. But what counts ethically is whether human needs come first — not whether the ultimate sanction is transcendental or secular.

What follows is a moral defense of euthanasia. Primarily I mean active or positive euthanasia, which helps the patient to die; not merely the passive or negative form of euthanasia which "lets the patient go" by simply withholding life-pre-serving treatments. The plain fact is that negative euthana-sia is already a fait accompli in modern medicine. Every day in a hundred hospitals across the land decisions are made clinically that the line has been crossed from prolonging genuinely human life to only prolonging subhuman dying, and when that judgment is made respirators are turned off, life-perpetuating intravenous infusions stopped, proposed surgery canceled, and drugs countermanded. So-called "Code 90" stickers are put on many record-jackets, indicat-ing "Give no intensive care or resuscitation." Arguing pro and con about negative euthanasia is therefore merely flogging a dead horse. Ethically, the issue whether we may "let the patient go" is as dead as Queen Anne.

Straight across the board of religious traditions there is substantial agreement that we are not morally obliged to preserve life in all terminal cases. (The religious-ethical defense of negative euthanasia is far more generally accept-ed by ministers and priests than medical people recognize or as yet even accept.) Humanist morality shows the same non-absolutistic attitude about preserving life. Indeed, not only Protestant, Catholic, and Jewish teaching take this stance; but it is also true of Buddhist, Hindu, and Moslem ethics. In short, the claim that we ought always to do everything we can to preserve any patient's life as long as possible is now discredited. ...

Given modern medicine's capabilities always to do what is technically possible to prolong life would be morally in-defensible on any ground other than a vitalistic outlook; that is, the opinion that biological survival is the first-order value and that all other considerations, such as personality, dignity, well-being, and self-possession, necessarily take second place. Vestigial last-ditch pro-vitalists still mumble threateningly about "what the Nazis did," but in fact the Nazis never engaged in euthanasia or mercy killing; what they did was merciless killing, either genocidal or for ruthless experimental purposes.

THE ETHICAL AND THE PRE-ETHICAL

One way of putting this is to say that the traditional ethics based on the sanctity of life — which was the classical doctrine of medical idealism in its prescientific phases — must give way to a code of ethics of the quality of life. This comes about for humane reasons. It is a result of modern medicine's successes, not failures. New occasions teach new duties, time makes ancient good uncouth, as Whittier said.
...

If God's will (perhaps "specially revealed" in the Bible or "generally revealed" in his Creation) is against any responsible human initiative in the dying process, or if· sheer life is believed to be, as such, more desirable than anything else, then those who hold these axioms will not find much merit in any case we might make for either kind of euthanasia — positive or negative. If, on the other hand, the highest good is personal integrity and human well-being, then euthanasia in either form could or might be the right thing to do, depending on the situation. This latter kind of ethics is the key to what will be said in this chapter.

Let's say it again, clearly, for the sake of truly serious ethical discourse. Many of us look upon living and dying as we do upon health and medical care, as person-centered. This is not a solely or basically biological understanding of what it means to be "alive" and to be "dead." It asserts that a so-called "vegetable," the brain-damaged victim of an auto accident or a microcephalic newborn or a case of massive neurologic deficit and lost cerebral capacity, who nevertheless goes on breathing and whose midbrain or brain stem continues to support spontaneous organ functions, is in such a situation no longer a human being, no longer a person, no longer really alive. It is personal function that counts, not biological function. Humanness is understood as primarily rational, not physiological. This "doctrine of man" puts the homo and ratio before the vita. It holds that being human is more "valuable" than being alive.

PLAYING GOD?

Using the old conventional conceptual apparatus, we naturally thought about both life and death as events, not as processes, which, of course, they are. We supposed that these events or episodes depended on the accidents of "nature" or on some kind of special providence. It is therefore no surprise to hear people grumbling that a lot of the decision making that has to be carried out in modern medical care is "playing God." And given that way of thinking the only possible answer to the charge is to accept it: "Yes, we are playing God." But the real question is: Which or whose God are we playing?

The old God who was believed to have a monopoly control of birth and death, allowing for no human responsibility in either initiating or terminating a life, was a primitive "God of the gaps" — a mysterious and awesome deity who filled in the gaps of our knowledge and of the control which our knowledge gives us. "He" was, so to speak, an hypothecation of human ignorance and helplessness.

In their growing up spiritually, men are now turning to a God who is the creative principle behind things, who is behind the test tube as much as the earthquake and volcano. This God can be believed in, but the old God's sacralistic inhibitions on human freedom and research can no longer be submitted to.

We must rid ourselves of that obsolete theodicy according to which God is not only the cause but also the builder of nature and its works, and not only the builder but even the manager. On this archaic basis it would be God himself who is the efficient as well as the final cause of earthquake and fire, of life and death, and by logical inference any "interference with nature" (which is exactly what medicine is) is "playing God." That God, seriously speaking, is dead.

All of this is said just to make it clear from the outset that biomedical progress is forcing us, whether we welcome it or not, to make fundamental conceptual changes as well as scientific and medical changes. Not only are the conditions of life and death changing, because of our greater control and in consequence our greater decision-making responsibility; our definitions of life and death also have to change to keep pace with the new realities. ...

CHOOSING DEATH

Genetics, molecular biology, fetology, and obstetrics have developed to a point where we now have effective control over the start of human life's continuum. And therefore from now on it would be irresponsible to leave baby-making to mere chance and impulse, as we once had to do. Modern men are trying to face up in a mature way to our emerging needs of quality control — medically, ecologically, legally, socially.

What has taken place in birth control is equally imperative in death control. The whole armory of resuscitation and prolongation of life forces us to be responsible decision makers about death as much as about birth; there must be quality control in the terminating of life as in its initiating. It is ridiculous to give ethical approval to the positive ending of subhuman life in utero, as we do in therapeutic abortions for reasons of mercy and compassion, but refuse to approve of positively ending a subhuman life in extremis. If we are morally obliged to put an end to a pregnancy when an amniocentesis reveals a terribly defective fetus, we are equally obliged to put an end to a patient's hopeless misery when a brain scan reveals that a patient with cancer has advanced brain metastases. ...

Only man is aware of death. Animals know pain, and fear it, but not death. Furthermore, in humans the ability to meet death and even to regard it sometimes as a friend is a sign of manliness. But in the new patterns of medicine and health care patients tend to die in a moribund or comatose state, so that death comes without the patient's knowledge. The Elizabethan litany's petition, "...from sudden death, good Lord, deliver us," has become irrelevant much if not most of the time.

It is because of this "incompetent" condition of so many of the dying that we cannot discuss the ethical issues of elective death only in the narrow terms of voluntary, patient-chosen

67

euthanasia. A careful typology of elective death will distinguish at least four forms — ways of dying which are not merely willy-nilly matters of blind chance but of choice, purpose, and responsible freedom. ...

1. Euthanasia, or a "good death," can be voluntary and direct, i.e., chosen and carried out by the patient. The most familiar way is the overdose left near at hand for the patient. It is a matter of simple request and of personal liberty. If it can be held in the abortion debate that compulsory pregnancy is unjust and that women should be free to control their own bodies when other's lives (fetuses) are at stake, do not the same moral claims apply to control of the lives and bodies of people too? In any particular case we might properly raise the question of the patient's competence, but to hold that euthanasia in this category is justifiable entails a rejection of the simplistic canard that all suicide victims are mentally disordered.

Voluntary euthanasia is, of course, a form of suicide. Presumably a related issue arises around the conventional notion of consent in medical ethics. The codes (American Medical Association, Helsinki, World Medical Association, Nuremberg) all contend that valid consent to any surgery or treatment requires a reasonable prospect of benefit to the patient. What, then, is benefit? Could death in some situations be a benefit? My own answer is in the affirmative.

2. Euthanasia can be voluntary but indirect. The choice might be made either in situ or long in advance of a terminal illness, e.g., by exacting a promise that if and when the "bare bodkin" or potion cannot be self-administered somebody will do it for the patient. In this case the patient gives to others — physicians, lawyers, family, friends — the discretion to end it all and when the situation requires, if the patient becomes comatose or too dysfunctioned to make the decision. ...

3. Euthanasia may be direct but involuntary. This is the form in which a simple "mercy killing" is done on a patient's behalf without his present or past request. Instances would be when an idiot is given a fatal dose or the death of a child in the worst stages of Tay-Sachs disease is speeded up, or when a man trapped inextricably in a blazing fire is shot to end his suffering, or a shutdown is ordered on a patient deep in mindless condition, irreversibly, perhaps due to an injury or an infection or some biological breakdown. ...

68

4. Finally, euthanasia might be both indirect and involuntary. This is the "letting the patient go" tactic which is taking place every day in our hospitals. Nothing is done for the patient positively to release him from his tragic condition (other than "trying to make him comfortable"), and what is done negatively is decided for him rather than in response to his request. ...

But ethically regarded, this indirect-involuntary form of euthanasia is manifestly superficial, morally timid, and evasive of the real issue. I repeat: it is harder morally to justify letting somebody die a slow and ugly death, dehumanized, than it is to justify helping him to avoid it.

MEANS AND ENDS

What, then, is the real issue? In a few words, it is whether we can morally justify taking it into our own hands to hasten death for ourselves (suicide) or for others (mercy killing) out of reasons of compassion. The answer to this in my view is clearly Yes, on both sides of it. Indeed, to justify either one, suicide or mercy killing, is to justify the other.

The heart of the matter analytically is the question of whether the end justifies the means. If the end sought is the patient's death as a release from pointless misery and dehumanization, then the requisite or appropriate means is justified. Immanuel Kant said that if we will the end we will the means. The old maxim of some moral theologians was finis sanctificat media. The point is that no act is anything but random and meaningless unless it is purposefully related to some end or object. To be moral an act must be seeking an end. ...

The really searching question of conscience is, therefore, whether we are right in believing that the well-being of persons is the highest good. If so, then it follows that either suicide or mercy killing could be the right thing to do in some exigent and tragic circumstances. This could be the case, for instance, when an incorrigible "human vegetable," whether spontaneously functioning or artificially supported, is progressively degraded while constantly eating up private or public financial resources in violation of the distributive justice owed to others. In such cases the patient is actually already departed and only his body is left, and the needs of others have a stronger claim upon us morally. ...

Another way of putting this is to say that the crucial question is not whether the end justifies the means (what else could?) but what justifies the end? And this chapter's answer is, plainly and confidently, that human happiness and well-being is the highest good or summum bonum, and that therefore any ends or purposes which that standard or ideal validates are just, right, good. This is what humanistic medicine is all about; it is what the concepts of loving concern and social justice are built upon. ...

The plain hard logic of it is that the end or purpose of both negative and positive euthanasia is exactly the same: to contrive or bring about the patient's death. Acts of deliberate omission are morally not different from acts of commission. But in the Anglo-American law, it is a crime to push a blind man off the cliff. It is not, however, a crime to deliberately not lift a finger to prevent his walking over the edge. ...

Careful study of the best texts of the Hippocratic Oath shows that it says nothing at all about preserving life, as such. It says that "so far as power and discernment shall be mine, I will carry out regimen for the benefit of the sick and will keep them from harm and wrong." The case for euthanasia depends upon how we understand "benefit of the sick" and "harm" and "wrong." If we regard dehumanized and merely biological life as sometimes real harm and the opposite of benefit, to refuse to welcome or even introduce death would be quite wrong morally.

In most states in this country people can and do carry cards, legally established (by Anatomical Gift Acts), which explain the carrier's wish that when he dies his organs and tissue should be used for transplant when needed by the living. The day will come when people will also be able to carry a card, notarized and legally executed, which explains that they do not want to be kept alive beyond the humanum point, and authorizing the ending of their biological processes by any of the methods of euthanasia which seems appropriate.

THE CASE AGAINST EUTHANASIA

Leonard J. Weber

Leonard J. Weber is an assistant professor in the religious studies department of Mercy College in Detroit, where he teaches Christian ethics and medical ethics. He is the author of **Christianity and War: Religious Ideas and Political Consequences**.

Think about the following questions while you read:

1. How does the author answer the question "What is a human person?" How is his answer important to the debate on euthanasia?
2. What position does the author take on the "sanctity of life" versus the "quality of life" controversy?
3. Why does the author feel that the principle that the end justifies the means is an inadequate basis for making a moral decision?

Leonard Weber, "Ethics and Euthanasia: Another View," **American Journal of Nursing**, July, 1973, pp. 1228-31. "Copyright July, 1973, The American Journal of Nursing Company. Reprinted from **American Journal of Nursing**. Condensed with permission of the American Journal of Nursing Company."

In his moral defense of euthanasia, Joseph Fletcher challenged many basic elements of the traditional ethical view of mercy killing. Such a challenge should not be unanswered; the matter is too important. ...

Personalistic Ethics

Dr. Fletcher argues that for anyone who accepts a personalistic and humanistic code of ethics, it is harder to justify letting someone die slowly than it is to give him a lethal injection. At the heart of his defense for directly killing certain patients who are terminally ill is his concept of a personalistic approach to ethics. This concept must be examined and seriously questioned.

Without a doubt, the human person must be the concern of ethics and medicine. The only proper care of a patient is to treat him as a person, a whole person, and not just as a specimen of biological life. A fundamental principle of medical ethics is that people be treated with respect; violation of the human person, thus, is unethical.

But what is a human person? A person is made up of components that are personal and physical, spiritual and corporeal. In traditional language a person is body and soul. The two cannot be separated in man as we know him. Man is an embodied being, the body of his spirit no less than the spirit of his body. The spirit may survive the death of the body, but the only person medicine ever knows is an embodied being. The human person, then, is violated when either the body or the personality is violated.

Ethicists like Dr. Fletcher appear to so emphasize the personality side of man that they tend to lose respect for the physical and to deny that a violation of the physical is a violation of the human person. ...

It is this neglect of the value of the physical dimension of man that is behind Dr. Fletcher's defense of direct euthanasia. He is right to advocate a personalistic ethic, but his notion of what constitutes a human person is too one-sided. A more adequate personalistic ethic would see the physical as worthy of respect. ... It would be most strange if the medical profession accepted a system of ethics that denies value to the body.

Mercy Killing and Allowing to Die

Ethicists who understand the person to be a combination of the spiritual and the physical are not particularly uneasy with the practice of allowing a terminally ill patient to die (not considering the question of who does the deciding), but they will have a great deal of uneasiness with directly taking the life of a patient to end his misery. In other words, the moral distinction between killing and allowing to die can be defended as valid and essential.

The starting point of medical ethics is proper respect for the human person. This implies the moral obligation to preserve health and prolong life. These obligations are not without limits, however. Just as a person should not be considered pure personality, so should he not be considered simply body. It is the good of the total man that must be served.

There is little doubt that terminally ill patients often are best served by giving up attempts to extend their lives and, instead, concentrating on their needs as dying persons. We miss the point, I think, when we see ending the prolongation of life simply in terms of death. Respect for a dying person may demand that we stop the art of healing so that we can help the patient practice what medieval man called ars moriendi, the art of dying. The positive meaning of "allowing the patient to die" is the attempt to provide for a peaceful death in the midst of family, rather than having a patient die alone, because the family may interfere with the staff's fight to keep death at bay. Actually, a good case can be made for initiating this type of care for patients earlier than is usually done.

Giving up the fight against death does not show lack of respect for the physical dimension of human personhood. It merely says that the overall good of the patient can best be served, not by violating the physical, but by allowing an illness or injury to take its course. The same cannot be said about directly intervening in order to bring about a good death. Mercy killing is not discontinuation of the fight to extend life in order to serve the needs of the dying patient. Rather, mercy killing is the direct ending of the life of the patient. As such, it is a violation of the person. It is a human agent, not a disease that is the immediate cause of death. This type of difference should not be ignored.

Dr. Fletcher advocates an ethics based upon an emphasis on the quality of life in opposition to the traditional ethics based upon the conviction of the sanctity of life. It is true

73

> **"I will neither give a deadly drug to anybody, if asked for, nor will I make a suggestion to this effect."**

From the **Hippocratic Oath**.

that there may be some difficulty with the sanctity-of-life concept, a difficulty that arises especially when we consider self-defense. Yet the basic elements of the sanctity-of-life ethics are essential for ethical living and cannot be set aside without weakening man's respect for man. Each person's life is sacred, beyond the realm of legitimate interference by another; all lives are of equal value. These are the primary premises of a sanctity-of-life ethics. There is no need to prove one's right to life and there is no justification for saying that the taking of one person's life is less of an evil than the taking of another's. Some such starting point would seem to be necessary if we are to respect a person because of the very fact that he is a person.

A quality-of-life ethics implies that only some lives are valuable and that only some lives are worthy of the respect that condemns physical violation. A quality-of-life ethics has an admirable goal: it sets out to improve the manner of human living. Yet it gets into trouble as soon as it opposes the quality of life against the sanctity of life. It immediately denies that the fact of human life is sufficient reason for inviolability; it ends by saying that some lives can be taken. ...

The sanctity-of-life approach is also concerned about the quality of human life. The quality of all our lives suffers, it insists, unless every human life is considered inviolable because of the very fact of its existence. A dying patient's relationship to those about him symbolizes the relationship of all men to one another. To practice direct euthanasia, even at the request of the patient, is to weaken the claim of each one of us to the right to have others respect and not violate us. Man is more than just spirit, and there are more ways of being violated than having one's free will coerced.

74

There is an enormous difference between not fighting death and actively putting an end to life. The former is fully compatible with respect for human life. The latter, while done with the best of intentions, is logically part of the view that human life itself is not enough to warrant our respect. The former is fully compatible with the humanistic nature of medicine itself. The latter could seem to be introducing a dehumanizing element into the medical profession.

Ends and Means

At the heart of the ethics of euthanasia lies the question of whether the end justifies the means. For Dr. Fletcher, the end (that is, purpose) most assuredly does justify the means. For this reason, euthanasia is considered good and for this reason there is no ethical difference between directly killing a patient and allowing him to die. In both cases, he contends, the end sought is the patient's release from pointless misery. This end is good and, therefore, the action necessary to bring about this end is also good. ...

The primary difficulty with this position is that the emphasis is on the purpose, the intention, the why of acting, and not enough on the nature of the action...

But acts have a moral quality, regardless of intention or purpose. Actions are not meaningless morally until purposely related to an end by man. By their very nature, actions produce consequences that often enhance or attack the well-being; the very action is evil. Now, intentions and circumstance are important. Killing in war, cold-blooded murder, and mercy killing are all different, morally speaking, because the circumstances are different. Yet there always is evil in the act of killing — the evil of rendering a previously alive person dead — and this evil is the starting point for all considerations of the morality of any kind of killing. ...

The principle that the proposed end justifies the means is found in a system of ethics that makes the mind of man the basis of morality. And to say that the mind of man is the basis of morality is to put man at the center of the meaning of the universe, a place which he does not truly occupy.

It sometimes seems as though there is a giant contradiction in the thinking of the modern Western world. In our understanding of the physical universe, we have experi-

> The principle that the proposed end justifies the means is found in a system of ethics that makes the mind of man the basis of morality. And to say that the mind of man is the basis of morality is to put man at the center of the meaning of the universe, a place which he does not truly occupy.

enced the Copernican revolution. In our understanding of the moral universe we are tending to do just the opposite: we are going from a world view that sees man as living morally by finding the meaning of the universe and conforming himself to it to the view that man himself, in his intentions, is the source and center of moral meaning. Fortunately, the moral reversal of the Copernican revolution is not accepted by all.

One does not have to believe in God in order to recognize that the meaning of the universe does not come from man's mind (though such a belief often helps). The recent ecological emphasis is, in part, an awareness of the fact that man is simply not being true to the facts when he acts as though he can give whatever meaning he wants to the world about him.

Modern medicine, with its tremendously increased ability to preserve life and restore health, has demonstrated the good that can be accomplished through science and technology. It must be careful, though, that it does not accept an attitude that often accompanies scientific and technological work: that nature has no meaning in itself and that such things as living and dying become meaningful in terms of human purpose and human control. The inadequacies and dangers of such an attitude are apparent.

When viewed in the context we have just been examining, direct euthanasia seems to be more closely related to prolonging life by all possible means than to allowing the patient to die.

Prolonging life as long as possible and directly bringing about death by mercy killing are both examples of attempts to control the living and dying processes to the greatest extent possible. Ceasing attempts to prolong life medically can, on the other hand, follow from quite a different attitude. What is being done in this case can be very much in tune with the idea that, at times, the most human way to act is to refuse to attempt to control life and death any further.

Just as human life does not have to prove its value by anyone's requirements for human personhood, so death does not have to be given meaning by the administration of a lethal injection at just the proper time. The decision not to resuscitate is fully compatible with respect for the fullness of human meaning. The administration of a lethal overdose is not.

ABILITY TO EMPATHIZE

The ability to empathize, to see life and its problems through another person's eyes, is a skill you must develop if you intend to learn from the experience of others.

Consider the following true life situation:

THE PREMATURE MONGOLOID*

Seven months along in her pregnancy, Mrs. Phyllis Obernauer woke up one morning feeling warm. She couldn't believe it, but she felt she was ready to deliver. As the Obernauers reached the hospital parking lot, Paul heard a gushing sound in the back seat. He turned around to see his baby daughter on the floor of the car.

For the next 24 hours, the hospital staff seemed to avoid her, Phyllis recalls, and even her obstetrician failed to visit her. She sensed something was wrong, but no one would say what. Finally, the crushing news: her premature daughter was not only mongoloid but had a hole in her heart and major intestinal blockage. The child gasped for every breath because of the heart problem and vomited everything it was fed because of the blockage. An operation would have to be performed immediately to correct the blockage or the baby would die.

"To me, this wasn't a birth, it was an ejection," Mrs. Obernauer, the mother of three other, healthy girls, says in a weary voice. "It was an imperfect fetus that my body wanted to get rid of. I looked ahead to the life this child would lead as a mongoloid, the expense of the hospitalization and the heart surgery someday. I looked at the terrific strain it would place on our girls and even more on our already shaky marriage, and I made a decision I didn't think I was capable of. I told them to let the baby die."

Phyllis recalls that the hospital staff was horrified by her attitude. "They hated me. But I would be the one saddled with this...this thing."

Her wish to allow the baby to die was not carried out. The local bureau of children's services obtained a court order and forced the intestinal operation. After $4,000 in bills, two months of intensive care — including intravenous feedings and massive doses of antibiotics to remedy a staph infection that blew up the baby's stomach like a balloon — the child was declared fit to go home.

"At first I wasn't going to pick her up from the hospital," Phyllis recalls. "But the word got around, and my 11-year-old daughter Audrey told me one of her friends had said, 'What a mommy you have. Won't even bring home her own baby.' " When the parents finally brought the child home, the Medicaid card issued read starkly, "OBERNAUER, BABY G." The Obernauers have steadfastly refused to name the baby, but call her Tara, after a character Phyllis saw on a soap opera.

Neighbors did their best to cheer Phyllis up. Some baked cookies, others brought toys for the baby, many spent hours sitting and talking. "One day I was introduced to this Presbyterian minister and I wondered why," she says. "Spiritual help? No, he had two mongoloid children and somehow I was supposed to see how blessed I was with one. But the children took to Tara and that's the toughest part. Just last night she had a hard time breathing and I found her in bed with Audrey this morning, with Holly — she's 9 — and Bonnie, 6, cooing over her.

"My husband's father was in a German concentration camp, so we Jews know to what extent 'mercy killings' can go. But why, when there are too many people in the world, keep alive an unwanted, malformed child? I've read all the books about mongoloid children, and the mothers tell of the love and affection and all. But it's like having a pet, not a human being. Many of the books conclude that death would be better."

Because of Phyllis's attitude, a social worker visited her new, sparsely furnished home in Chester, N.J. once a month for about half a year to make sure she didn't mistreat the baby. "What can my children think of their mother when

this state car pulls up to check on her?'' she says. ''The bureaucracy, the state make me sick. I told them they saved the baby, they could keep her. But if they institutionalize the baby, we'd have to pay $200 a month. My husband just lost his drugstore business and we're just barely making it now.'' Paul Obernauer, who works as a pharmacist, and his wife have had stormy months since the child was born. In the anguish and confusion, each has blamed the other for the child and they have seriously considered divorce. ...

A doctor recently recommended that the baby might be helped by an experimental muscle-strengthening drug, but Phyllis refuses to consider it. "I'll do no more for the child than clean and feed and dress her.

"We don't think what it will be like a year or even a month from now. In one sense I'm sitting at home waiting for this child to die. If she gets pneumonia I don't think I'd rush her to the hospital. But that's tougher to say as each day goes by. The decision to let a child like this die must be made — and respected — before there is any attachment. But I still say, if there was a place where I could take this child today and she would be put to sleep permanently, I would do it."

INSTRUCTIONS

Try to imagine how the following individuals would react to this situation.
What reasons do you think they would give for their actions?
Try to imagine and explain their feelings.

Mrs. Obernauer

Mr. Obernauer

Tara's sisters

Tara at the age of 16 (if she lives)

Mrs. Obernauer's doctor

The hospital staff

The authors of "The Aborting Society" (reading #4)

Joseph Fletcher (Author of reading #11)

Leonard Weber (Author of reading #12)

YOU

CAPITAL PUNISHMENT

"THOU SHALT NOT KILL"

U.S. SUPREME COURT

THE DEATH PENALTY IS "CRUEL AND UNUSUAL PUNISHMENT"

ORGANIZED SOCIETY

THE CASE AGAINST THE DEATH PENALTY

Hugo A. Bedau

Hugo A. Bedau is the editor and author of the books **The Death Penalty in America** and **Justice and Equality**, among other works. He is President of the American League to Abolish Capital Punishment and is a professor of philosophy at Tufts University, Medford, Massachusetts. His statement was taken from a pamphlet distributed by the American Civil Liberties Union, **The Case Against the Death Penalty**. The ACLU was founded in 1920 to champion the rights of man as set forth in the Declaration of Independence and the Constitution.

Use the following questions to assist your reading:

1. On what points did the majority of the Supreme Court agree in its historic case Furman vs. Georgia which ruled against capital punishment in the U.S.?
2. What three points does the author make in arguing against the death penalty?
3. What proof does the author present to support his claim that there is racial bias in the use of the death penalty?

Hugo A. Bedau, **The Case Against the Death Penalty**, a pamphlet dated January, 1973, distributed by the American Civil Liberties Union.

The Supreme Court has, in effect, outlawed capital punishment in the United States by its decision in Furman v. Georgia. Because of Furman, by the end of 1972, nearly two dozen states had overturned their death penalty statutes and ordered resentencing of persons awaiting execution. The ACLU, with the NAACP Legal Defense and Educational Fund, Inc. and other civil liberties and civil rights organizations, has properly pointed to the Furman decision as the watershed in its long struggle against capital punishment.

In the immediate aftermath of the Court's decision, many commentators made much of the narrowness of the victory and the lack of firm consensus among the five-man majority on the Court. This is understandable — but misleading. It obscures several major points of agreement:

* The majority agreed that the death penalty is a cruel and unusual punishment because it is imposed infrequently and under no clear standards.

* The majority agreed that the purpose of the death penalty, whether it be retribution or deterrence, cannot be achieved when it is so rarely and unpredictably used.

* The majority agreed that one purpose of the Eighth and Fourteenth Amendments is to bar legislatures from imposing punishments like the death penalty which, because of the way they are administered, serve no valid social purpose.

* All the Court, with the exception of Justice Rehnquist, indicated personal opposition to capital punishment.

* All the Court, again excepting Justice Rehnquist, indicated substantial belief that capital sentencing is arbitrary and substantial disbelief that it is uniquely effective in deterring crime.

The ACLU's opposition to the death penalty has been based on several grounds, including those which the Court found compelling:

* Capital punishment is cruel and unusual, in violation of the Eighth Amendment of the U.S. Constitution. It is a relic of the earliest days of penology, when slavery, branding and other corporal punishments were commonplace; like these other barbaric practices, it has no place in civilized society.

* Executions in prison gave the unmistakable message to all society that life ceases to be sacred when it is thought useful to take it and that violence is legitimate so long as it is thought justified by pragmatic concerns that appeal to those having power to kill.

* Capital punishment denies due process of law. Its imposition is arbitrary, and it forever deprives an individual of the benefits of new law or new evidence that might affect his conviction.

* The worst and most dangerous criminals are rarely the ones executed. The death penalty is applied randomly at best and discriminatorily at worst. It violates the constitutional guarantee of the equal protection of the laws because it is imposed almost exclusively against racial minorities, the poor, the uneducated — persons who are victims of overt discrimination in the sentencing process or who are unable to afford expert and dedicated legal counsel.

* Reliance on the death penalty obscures the true causes of crime and distracts attention from the effective resources of society to control it.

* Capital punishment is wasteful of resources, demanding a disproportionate expenditure of time and energy by courts, prosecuting attorneys, defense attorneys, juries, courtroom and correctional personnel; it burdens the system of criminal justice, and it is counter-productive as an instrument for society's control of violent crime. It uniquely epitomizes the tragic inefficacy and brutality of a resort to violence rather than reason for the solution of difficult social problems.

Two facts — plainly recognized by the majority of the Supreme Court in Furman — buttress our entire case: capital punishment does not deter crime, and the administration of the death penalty has been provably unfair.

Deterrence

The argument against the deterrent efficacy of the death penalty takes three mutually supportive forms.

1. Any punishment can be an effective deterrent only if it is consistently and promptly employed. Capital punishment does not meet those conditions. Only a small proportion of first degree murderers are sentenced to death, and even fewer are executed. Between 1930 and 1960, there was one execution for every 70 homicides. During the decade 1951-1960, nine out of ten persons convicted of first degree murder did not get executed; and in the decade of the '60's executions became still rarer. The delay in carrying out the death sentence has become notorious. Between 1961 and 1970, the average time spent under death sentence rose from 14.4 months to 32.6 months. The sobering lesson is that we must either abolish the death penalty or try to enhance its deterrent efficacy by abandoning the procedural safeguards and constitutional rights of suspects, defendants and convicts in order to reduce delay (with the attendant high risk of executing innocent persons). The former alternative is surely the only tolerable one: Repeal the death penalty entirely in favor of a more efficiently administrable mode of punishment.

Nothing emerges from the study of trends in violent crimes in Canada that would support or even suggest the proposition that the suspension of capital punishment has caused an increase in the homicide rate.

From a Canadian government study on capital punishment, conducted by Ezzat Abdel Fattah, a Montreal criminologist.

2. Persons who commit murder and other crimes of personal violence either premeditate them or they do not. If they do not, then the requisite mens rea (criminal intent) of a capital crime is missing; and it is impossible to imagine how in such cases any punishment could deter. In cases where the crime is premeditated, the criminal ordinarily expects to escape detection, arrest and conviction. It is impossible to see how the threat of a severe punishment can deter an individual who does not expect to get caught. Gangland killings, air piracy, kidnapping for ransom are among the more obvious categories of capitally punishable crimes which continue to occur because some think they are too clever to get caught.

86

3. Experience over the past three decades tends to establish that the death penalty as currently administered is no more effective than imprisonment in deterring crime and that it may even be an incitement to criminal violence:

A. Use of the death penalty in a given state does not decrease the subsequent rate of criminal homicide in that state.

B. Use of the death penalty in a given state may increase the subsequent rate of criminal homicide in that state.

C. Death penalty states as a group do not have lower rates of criminal homicide than non-death penalty states.

D. States that abolish the death penalty do not show an increased rate of criminal homicide after abolition.

E. States that have reinstituted the death penalty after abolishing it have not shown a decreased rate of criminal homicide.

F. In two neighboring states — one with the death penalty and the other without it — the one with the death penalty does not show any consistently lower rate of criminal homicide.

G. Police officers on duty do not suffer a higher rate of criminal assault and homicide in states that have abolished the death penalty than they do in death penalty states.

H. Prisoners and prison personnel do not suffer a higher rate of criminal assault and homicide from life-term prisoners in abolition states than they do in death penalty states.

Actual experience establishes these conclusions beyond reasonable doubt. No comparable body of evidence contradicts these views.

In addition, an increasing number of cases have been clinically documented where the death penalty actually incited the capital crimes that it was supposed to deter. These included cases of the so-called suicide-murder syndrome — persons who wanted but feared to take their own lives, and committed murder so that society would kill them — and the so-called executioner syndrome — persons who became the self-appointed ministers of death and used the ultimate weapon legitimated by society's acceptance of capital punishment to avenge real or fancied wrongs. Indeed, the more that is known about the mind of murderers, the more obvious it becomes that the picture of a rational and calculated decision to kill upon which the supposed deterrent efficacy of capital punishment entirely depends is almost never encountered in actual life.

Justus in the **Minneapolis Star**, reprinted with permission.

Unfairness

Constitutional due process as well as elementary justice require that the judicial functions of trial and sentencing, especially where the irreversible sanction of the death penalty is involved, be conducted with fundamental fairness. In both rape and murder cases (since 1930, 99 per cent of all executions have been for these crimes), there has been substantial evidence to show that courts have been arbitrary, racially biased and unfair in the way in which they have tried and sentenced some persons to prison and others to death.
...

Since 1930, 3,859 persons have been executed in the United States. Of these, 2,066, or 54 per cent, were black. For the crime of murder, 3,334 have been executed; 1,630, or 49 per cent, were black. During these years blacks were about one-eleventh of the population. For rape, punishable by death in 1972 in only sixteen states and by the federal government, a total of 455 have been executed, all but two in the South; 405, or 90 per cent, were black.

More exact statistical studies show that the higher rate of executions of blacks for rape and homicide cannot be explained by any factor except the race of the defendant. ...

Race is not the only morally and legally invidious factor which in practice plays a role in determining who gets executed and who does not. A defendant's poverty, lack of firm social roots in the community, inadequate legal representation at trial or on appeal — all these have in the past been common factors among "Death Row" populations. Race, however, has proved to be the most influential of them all. There is no reason to believe that were capital punishment once again permitted, it would prove to be less discriminatory in the future than it has been in the past. ...

ACLU Position

The ACLU takes the position that the moral and legal principles and the array of factual evidence that persuaded the majority of the Supreme Court in 1972 to rule against the death penalty as currently administered destroy the basis for reintroduction of the death penalty in any form for any crime. The death penalty, we believe, continues to be the symbolic representation of everything that is brutal and futile in our present system of criminal justice. We cannot rest until it is thoroughly uprooted and eliminated from our law.

ARGUMENTS FOR THE DEATH PENALTY

by Ernest Van Den Haag

Ernest Van Den Haag is a professor of social philosophy at New York University. He also lectures on psychology and sociology at the New School of Social Research and maintains a private practice in psychoanalysis. His books include **The Fabric of Society**, **Education As An Industry**, **The Jewish Mystique** and **Passion and Social Constraint**.

Think of the following questions while you read:

1. Why does Mr. Van Den Haag think that the disproportionate number of blacks being executed is not a valid argument against capital punishment?
2. How does the author react to the argument that the death penalty is unconstitutional because it constitutes cruel and unusual punishment?
3. What point does Mr. Van Den Haag make when he states "if we fail to execute, we may have failed to add the deterrent that might have prevented prospective murderers from engaging in murder?"

From testimony given on March 15, 1972, before Subcommittee No. 3 of the House Committee on the Judiciary in the course of hearings on pending bills proposing suspension or abolition of the death penalty.

There are a variety of reasons given for suspending the death penalty or finally eliminating it. One of the reasons offered is the undenied fact that more blacks are executed than whites. Yet this would suggest discrimination only if it could be shown that fewer whites, equally convicted, are executed. It is not enough to show that more blacks are executed. We would have to show that a higher proportion of convicted blacks are executed. I find no trace of that in the statistics presented.

But if the statistics did show discrimination — which I do not think they do — then, that discrimination would be in the distribution of the penalty in question, the death penalty, and would not be inherent in the nature of the penalty. Such discrimination might be equally claimed for all other penalties. The claim would be probably as true, or as false, as it is for the death penalty. It would then be up to Congress not just to suspend the death penalty, but also to suspend the penalty of imprisonment, which is equally discriminatory. ...

The death penalty is irrevocable. No penalty is reversible, of course. But the death penalty in addition to not being reversible is also irrevocable. And, of course, for this reason, we have to make particularly sure that it is inflicted both sparingly and with great discrimination.

A second suggestion is that the death penalty is unusual within the constitutional meaning of that term. Now obviously, the writers of the Constitution did not mean to exclude the death penalty which certainly was usual in their day.

But in the last 10 years, although still imposed fairly frequently by the courts in many States, the death penalty has not been applied often, owing to judicial reviews and in some cases to the intervention of Governors. These activities have been the cause, and not the effect of the nonapplication or unusualness.

The judiciary or the political office holders who by their activities have made the death penalty "unusual" cannot thereupon turn around and use the unusualness which they have produced as an argument to ban or suspend the penalty because it has become unusual. They have made it so.

To argue thereupon that the death penalty should be suspended or abolished is clearly to parody the intent of the

Constitution. That intent was to exclude penalties that an eccentric judge might impose and which would not usually be imposed for the crime involved. Or, penalties which have not been imposed by common consent for a lengthy period. I find no such common consent in this country. Or, finally, penalties newly legislated which are contrary to our legal tradition. Certainly, this would not apply here either.

If it were put to referendum in any of the States where it has been abolished, it is my guess that the majority would be in favor of retention of the death penalty. But I certainly think it would be a good idea to have such a vote.

REINSTATING CAPITAL PUNISHMENT

If your state does wish to reinstate capital punishment, the consensus of attorneys general is that it should specify death for the following crimes: for the murder of a police officer, a corrections officer, or a fireman on duty.

Murder by a hired killer.

Murder by malicious use of a bomb.

Murder by a person convicted previously of murder.

Murder by any person under life imprisonment.

Murder committed during a rape.

Murder resulting from the hijacking of any public vehicle.

Multiple slayings.

Murder of a public official.

These crimes your state can discourage now.

Paul Harvey, "The Death Penalty Should Be Restored," **Human Events**, July 28, 1973.

It is also suggested that the death penalty is cruel in the constitutional meaning of that term. Standards of cruelty vary historically. There is, however, no evidence to my knowledge that the majority of Americans now regard the death penalty as cruel.

Death, and the expectation of death are certainly natural phenomena. They cannot be regarded as cruel within the constitutional meaning of the term.

What can be regarded as cruel is a particularly painful way of inflicting death. And I take it that is what the Constitution might have had in mind, a particularly cruel way of punishing a person or a particularly undeserved death, which we usually regard as cruel.

The death penalty meets neither of these criteria and cannot be regarded as "cruel" therefore.

The general purposes of the death penalty are (1) justice. It may well be that failure to impose the death penalty will outrage the sense of justice of the community so as to weaken respect for law. If a life sentence is substituted, it would mean that the relatives of a murder victim will have to support the murderer through their taxes for the rest of his life. I can't imagine that they would welcome this.

A second general purpose of the death penalty is deterrence of others. There is a great deal of confusion on this issue. And I cannot flatter myself that I will be able to clear it up. But I would like to make a few suggestions.

All penalties — including fines, prison sentences and the death penalty — are deterrent roughly in proportion to their severity, all other things being equal. Were that not the case, we would certainly not have varied penalties but might impose a uniform penalty of $5 for any crime whatsoever. We impose penalties roughly differentiated, because we feel that crimes of different gravity deserve different punishment, both in terms of justice and in terms of their importance as deterrents.

The question is whether the severity added by the death penalty adds enough deterrence to warrant inflicting it. In practical terms the question is whether potential murderers are deterred by the threat of a life sentence. That is, I think, the basic and essential question.

DEATH PENALTY IS AN EFFECTIVE DETERRENT

The sharp reduction in the application of the death penalty was a component of the more permissive attitude toward crime in the last decade.

I do not contend that the death penalty is a panacea that will cure crime. Crime is the product of a variety of different circumstances — sometimes social, sometimes psychological — but it is committed by human beings and at the point of commission it is the product of that individual's motivation. If the incentive not to commit crime is stronger than the incentive to commit it, then logic suggests that crime will be reduced. It is in part the entirely justified feeling of the prospective criminal that he will not suffer for his deed which, in the present circumstances, helps allow those deeds to take place.

Federal crimes are rarely "crimes of passion." Airplane hi-jacking is not done in a blind rage; it has to be carefully planned. Using incendiary devices and bombs are not crimes of passion, nor is kidnapping; all these must be thought out in advance. At present those who plan these crimes do not have to include in their deliberations the possibility that they will be put to death for their deeds. I believe that in making their plans, they should have to consider the fact that if a death results from their crime, they too may die. ...

Hard experience has taught us that with due regard for the rights of all — including the right to life itself — we must return to a greater concern with protecting those who might otherwise be the innocent victims of violent crime than with protecting those who have committed those crimes. The society which fails to recognize this as a reasonable ordering of its priorities must inevitably find itself, in time, at the mercy of criminals.

President Richard M. Nixon, March 14, 1973 State of the Union Message on crime and law enforcement.

Those who feel that the death penalty has no additional deterrent effect rest their case on two arguments.

First, they contend that statistics do not clearly show a special deterrent effect of the death penalty. I think this is correct. It must be noted, however, that there are no statistics showing a clear deterrent effect of any penalty. Nonetheless, it is generally felt, and reasonably so, that a more severe penalty is likely to be more deterrent than a less severe one, all other things being equal. All other things seldom are equal. Therefore, a strict demonstration of deterrence is unlikely to be forthcoming.

Statistics, whether they do show a rise of capital crimes after abolition (some statistics do) or not (some statistics do not), are not helpful. If a rise of capital crimes has occurred, it may have been due to factors other than abolition. If a decline has occurred, it might have been greater had the death penalty been retained. (The same is true for any other penalty).

The absence of proof for the additionally deterrent effect of the death penalty must not be confused with the presence of proof for the absence of this effect. On the basis of the statistics available, no logical conclusion one way or the other can be reached. It cannot be proven that the death penalty is additionally deterrent; it cannot be proved either that it is not.

The second argument against the death penalty usually offered is that the overwhelming number of capital crimes are acts of irrational passion committed among acquaintances and relatives and are unlikely to be influenced by any threatened penalty. Many of these acts , it is suggested, are committed by somewhat irrational persons.

If the data be true the argument based on them is, nonetheless, without merit. If most capital crimes are commited by irrational persons, chances are that rational persons have been deterred so far by the death penalty, and would no longer be deterred if it were abolished.

No penalty can deter the irrational, perhaps. But penalties do influence those who are rational enough to be influenced. In this respect the data suggest the death penalty has been very effective, precisely because very few murders are committed by rational persons.

Since we do not know for certain whether or not the death penalty adds deterrence, we have in effect the choice of two risks.

Risk 1. —If we execute convicted murderers, without thereby deterring prospective murderers beyond the deterrence that could have been obtained by life imprisonment, we may have vainly sacrificed the life of the convicted murderers.

Risk 2. — If we fail to execute a convicted murderer whose execution might have deterred an indefinite number of prospective murderers, our failure sacrifices an indefinite number of victims of future murderers. The lives of these victims could have been spared had the convicted murderer been executed.

Let me paraphrase this once more. The statistics are such that we simply are confronted with two risks. We may execute without thereby adding to deterrence and vainly sacrifice the life of the executed murderer. But if we fail to execute, we may have failed to add the deterrent that might have prevented prospective murderers from engaging in murder. We may therefore have been sacrificing the lives of victims who might have been spared, had we executed the convicted man.

If we had certainty, we would not have risks. We do not have certainty. If we have risks, and we do, I would rather risk the life of the convicted man than risk the life of an indefinite number of innocent victims who might survive if he were executed.

So, I urge you neither to suspend nor to abolish the death penalty.

ABILITY TO DISCRIMINATE

Recently, the Harris Survey asked a nationwide cross section of 1,537 households this question, repeated from previous years:

"Do you believe in capital punishment (death penalty) or are you opposed to it?"

	1969	1970	1973
Believe in	48%	47%	59%
Opposed	38	42	31
Not sure	14	11	10

Usually difficult situations fail to present easy choices. Real life problems are too complex to permit simple choices between absolute right and wrong. The following exercise will test your ability to discriminate between degrees of truth and falsehood by completing the questionnaire. Circle the number on the continuum which most closely identifies your evaluation regarding each statement's degree of truth or falsehood.

1. All multiple murderers should be executed in fairness to their potential future victims.

```
+ ____5_4_3_2_1_0_1_2_3_4_5____ —
    completely  partially  partially  completely
       true        true      false      false
```

97

2. Reliance on the death penalty obscures the true causes of crime and distracts attention from the effective resources of society to control it.

+ | 5 4 3 2 1 0 1 2 3 4 5 | –

completely   partially   partially   completely
true   true   false   false

3. The problem with capital punishment today is not the principle itself, but the inability of man to administer it wisely.

+ | 5 4 3 2 1 0 1 2 3 4 5 | –

completely   partially   partially   completely
true   true   false   false

4. Support for the death penalty indicates an anti-life, vindictive nature inconsistent with the gospel.

+ | 5 4 3 2 1 0 1 2 3 4 5 | –

completely   partially   partially   completely
true   true   false   false

5. A government which cannot execute criminals will lose respect, and a permissive and irresponsible society will be the result.

+ | 5 4 3 2 1 0 1 2 3 4 5 | –

completely   partially   partially   completely
true   true   false   false

6. Capital punishment can be a very effective deterrent for premeditated crimes such as airplane hijacking and kidnapping.

+ | 5 4 3 2 1 0 1 2 3 4 5 | –

completely   partially   partially   completely
true   true   false   false

7. Capital punishment, like corporal punishment, branding, slavery and other barbaric practices has no place in a civilized society.

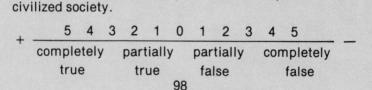

+ | 5 4 3 2 1 0 1 2 3 4 5 | –

completely   partially   partially   completely
true   true   false   false

A SCRIPTURAL BASIS
FOR THE DEATH PENALTY

William F. Dankenbring

Mr. Dankenbring is currently an associate editor of **Plain Truth** magazine. He has a master's degree in theology from Ambassador College in Pasadena, California, and his book **The Creation-Evolution Controversy** will be published in the near future.

As you read try to answer the following questions:

1. Where are the first references in the Bible to God permitting the use of the death penalty?
2. How does the author answer the objection to the death penalty that innocent men will occasionally be executed?
3. What does the author mean when he says that "the problem with capital punishment today is not the principle itself?"

Joseph Bernard Morse, at age 20, murdered his mother and sister. His mother, 58 years old, was beaten to death with a rock. His 12-year-old sister, who was crippled with cystic fibrosis, was smothered with pillows and beaten with a ball bat and a rock.

Morse was convicted of first degree murder and sentenced to death. But because of a legal technicality, the conviction was overturned and a retrial ordered. A new jury gave the accused life imprisonment. Eight days later Morse killed again. This time the victim was a fellow inmate in jail.

Proponents of capital punishment argue that if Morse had been executed after his first conviction, a life could have been saved.

In another case, a woman was raped in the basement of an apartment house while doing her laundry. A suspect was questioned, submitted to a lie detector test, and after questioning, he admitted the crime. He later repeated his confession and dictated it to a typist. But because of a legal technicality, he was released from jail. A few years later he raped again.

How should society deal with such crimes — by sentencing those guilty to death? But what about the other problem of possibly putting the wrong man to death? ...

The controversy rages. Opinions are sharply divided. How, then, can we reach the proper conclusion? Should capital punishment be abolished everywhere? Is the death penalty inherently ineffective? Is it a barbarous anachronism in our modern world?

Both sides commonly cite the Bible in support of their particular views. Some claim the Bible advocates capital punishment. Others say that since God is a God of mercy and love, capital punishment is not a suitable penalty for serious crime. Since both sides often cite the Bible to bolster their opinions, we ought to look into the Bible and see what it really says on this issue.

What does the scriptural record say regarding capital punishment? You may be surprised.

The First Murder

In the dawn of human civilization, asserts the Biblical record, a man named Cain rose up and murdered his brother, Abel, in a fit of rage (Gen. 4:1-8). What was the punishment which God imposed on Cain for this first record-ed homicide? Interestingly, it was not the death penalty!

Rather, as you read the account, you will discover that Cain was banished from society — exiled into the wilderness of Nod (verses 9-16). In this case, God allowed Cain to live; the world's first murderer was not put to death.

After those days, according to the Biblical account, men began to multiply on the earth. And soon there followed the second recorded murder in history, when Lamech, a descen-dant of Cain, slew a young man who apparently had fought with him (Gen. 4:23). No mention is made of Lamech being put to death for his homicide (verse 24).

But as men began to multiply, the earth became filled with increasing violence (Gen. 6:1, 11-12). A cursory study of the Biblical account shows that, in the absence of a death penalty for crimes, the earth became FILLED with violence! One might conclude that since criminals were not speedily executed or dealt with appropriately, the world experienced a spiraling crime epidemic!

A New Order

Such were the conditions which prevailed before the deluge according to the Biblical account. Soon after the deluge, the Bible continues, God determined that human beings, who wanted their own governments, would be granted the right, or authority, to execute those guilty of murder. You can read the account in Genesis 9, beginning in verse 5: "And I will avenge the shedding of your own life-blood; I will avenge it on any beast, I will avenge man's life on man, upon his brother-man; whoever sheds human blood, by human hands shall his own blood be shed — for God made man in his own likeness" (verses 5-6, Moffatt).

God, as the Creator of man, and as the supreme life-giver, has authority to take one's life if it is misused or abused (Deut.32:39). So we read that after the deluge, God also permitted human government — human beings — the use of the death penalty for particular crimes.

Capital Punishment in Ancient Israel

When ancient Israel came out of Egypt, they received a system of laws, statutes and ordinances, based on the Ten

Commandments (Exodus 20). The Bible implicitly says God gave these laws to Israel.

Was capital punishment a part of that system of laws? In Exodus 21:12 we read: "He who strikes a man, so that he dies, must be put to death." Further, in verse 14, we read: "Only if one man wilfully attacks another, to murder him craftily, you must take that man from my very altar and put him to death." Capital punishment was decreed and enforced!

Obviously, the death penalty for capital offenses was NOT considered "cruel or unusual punishment" by the early writers of the Bible. It was a part of the law enforcement procedure given to ancient Israel.

Executions were carried out publicly. The witnesses themselves, after a person was convicted by the judges, participated in carrying out the punishment. Thus other would-be criminals would "hear and fear" to commit the same crimes (see Joshua 7:19-26).

And it worked. As long as the laws of God were enforced, the people of Israel had peace and safety (see Joshua 24:31). The shock of public executions for major crimes caused people to obey the laws as long as they were enforced. But when enforcement began to lag and sentences were no longer speedily carried out, the result was a crime explosion. As the historical book of Judges records: "In those days there was no king in Israel, but every man did that which was right in his own eyes" (Judges 17:6; 21:25).

The principle of speedy punishment was impressed upon King Solomon, reputed in the Bible to be the wisest king of his day. He gave his attention to the problem of crime and punishment, and concluded: "Because sentence on a crime is not executed at once, the mind of man is prone to evil practices" (Eccl. 8:11, Moffatt).

Notice that Solomon was aware of two principles involved in curtailing crime: First, sentence must be executed to be effective; it is not enough merely to be on the lawbooks. And secondly, it must be carried out swiftly, not subjected to interminable delays until the crime is finally forgotten and no longer seems important.

But what about the execution of innocent persons? Surely here the death penalty is a terrible miscarriage of justice.

> **Should a man dare to kill his fellow by treacherous intent, you must take him even from my altar to be put to death.**

Exodus 21:14

The Other Side of the Issue

Surely, one of the worst crimes is to inflict the death penalty on an innocent person. This has been done in the past. It has been done in the present.

One such case is recorded in the Old Testament of the Bible. King Ahab of Israel coveted the vineyard of a certain Naboth, who lived adjoining the king's palace. Naboth, however, refused to sell his property to Ahab.

Jezebel, Ahab's wicked wife, plotted to obtain the vineyard for her husband, and wrote letters in the king's name to the elders of the city, telling them to set two false accusers to testify that Naboth had blasphemed God and the king. The men of the city followed the instructions, and Naboth was stoned with stones until he died (see I Kings 21:1-14).

God, however, was not pleased with this turn of affairs and sent His prophet to warn Ahab and Jezebel that He would hold them accountable for their reprehensible conduct — He would require their blood for that of Naboth's (verses 17-25). The retribution was fulfilled soon thereafter in a civil and a foreign war (see I Kings 22:34-38; II Kings 9:30-37).

This illustration shows there is a definite risk in the carrying out of capital punishment. God knew men would at times misuse this authority, and that rulers, judges and juries would, mistakenly or intentionally, put to death innocent men (see II Kings 21:16). God holds those so involved accountable for the abuse of their power (verses 11-15).

The Abuse of Power

What we must realize is that God has given human nations and governments power to decree laws and to punish evildoers (Romans 13:1-6). He has given nations and governments during this present age the authority to execute criminals, to inflict the death penalty for major crimes.

But that authority is not a one-way street.

He will hold those who exercise this power accountable for how fairly and equitably they use their authority.

Those in seats of power and positions of rulership must realize their awesome responsibility. As King David said thousands of years ago: "He that ruleth over men must be just, ruling in the fear of God" (II Samuel 23:3). How true that is! Those who abuse their power or fail to properly exercise it when they ought to do so will be held responsible for the consequences.

Unfortunately, most nations today go to one of two extremes. Some are saddled with a system of interminable judicial delays and are abandoning capital punishment because it thus ceases to have a significant deterrent effect. Other nations are using the death penalty to remove those who disagree with the established regime, who are supposedly guilty of "political crimes." Both extremes lead to disastrous consequences — an explosive crime rate on the one hand, or a police state on the other.

A Complex Issue

The question of capital punishment is a thorny issue, deeply entwined with many other social issues.

When capital punishment is interminably delayed, needless mental torment and anguish are caused. When it is not carried out impartially as to race, creed, or economic status, the result is growing hostility and alienation among those discriminated against.

To be effective, capital punishment must be administered impartially. And it must be administered swiftly, while the memory of the crime is still strong in the public's mind — as soon as possible after the criminal is apprehended and convicted of the crime.

If these principles were followed, the crime rate would be dramatically reduced. Nations would also be saved the incalculable expense of maintaining prisons and providing for the needs and sustenance of men who had committed crimes worthy of death. ...

An Alternative to the Death Penalty

Is there a workable alternative in today's world to capital punishment for serious crime?

After examining the Scriptural record, we find that the Bible is quite clear. Although nations may attempt to abolish the death penalty, the Bible makes plain that there are certain cases where no other penalty is suitable. In the case of hardened, incorrigible criminals — those who will not repent of their crimes — no other penalty will solve the problem. If released from prison, such criminals will return to crime, and perhaps rape or murder again. Such criminals deserve the death penalty.

For those who are guilty of such heinous crimes and deserve death, but who, from the heart, repent, and who bring forth unmistakable evidence in their attitudes and lives that they have truly repented, the Bible does provide an alternative for the death penalty. That alternative is forgiveness — pardon — grace!

If a man repents of his past deeds, and proves by his life that he has truly changed, then God no longer holds his past deeds against him. In the New Testament, this act of mercy is called "grace," meaning "pardon."

This is the approach and example our modern society itself ought to follow. ...

The Inability of Man

The problem with capital punishment today is not the principle itself, but the inability of man cut off from God to administer it fairly, wisely, righteously. Larger issues emerge. Does man of himself have the capacity to be absolutely just, fair, and equitable? Do humans have the innate ability to judge righteously?

Even when sincere men try their best, can they be utterly confident that they haven't made a mistake? What man has the ability to look into the human heart and to judge with absolute fairness? In some cases the answer may appear clear cut — but what about borderline cases? ...

The point is simply this: Human beings — weak, fallible, emotional, shortsighted, prejudiced as they often are — are simply unable to always execute true justice and judgment!

Where does this leave us?

True Justice

This fact ought to teach us a fundamental lesson — that man ought not look to himself to bring justice to the earth. He ought to look outside himself — above himself — to God, the Creator.

THE DEATH PENALTY
IS INCONSISTENT
WITH THE GOSPEL

the National Catholic Reporter

The National Catholic Reporter is a weekly newspaper published and written by a group of Catholic lay people. The following reading appeared as an editorial.

The following questions should help you examine the reading:

1. Why, according to this editorial, have theologians taken a position against the death penalty?
2. What are the reasons given for the current interest in reviving the death penalty?
3. Why is the claim made that the death penalty is inconsistent with the gospel?

From an editorial in the April 6, 1973 issue of **The National Catholic Reporter**. Reprinted with permission.

Catholic theology has come to see that reverence for life means not just the unborn, not just the innocent, but even the most guilty — even the least of our brethren.

The death penalty, theologians have realized, prevents a person from his right to penance and sorrow, and excuses society from its responsibility to rehabilitate.

There are a number of other reasons for opposing the death penalty:

* The chief argument for the death penalty, that it acts as a deterrent to further capital crimes, has been proved false. The death penalty has not reduced such crimes, and although it has been enforced inequitably, affecting the poor more than the affluent, the argument that applying the death penalty more equitably will make it a better deterrent does not seem strong. ...The traditional notion of deterrence itself is weak because the death penalty has not been proved to be the best and most ethical deterrent, and because of depersonalizing people by making them examples creates moral problems in itself.

* For a penalty to be effective, it must be understood rationally by the person who brings it on himself, and those who commit capital crimes are less rational than most, less capable of understanding what they are doing. This does not condone those acts, but it shows that death is not the best solution.

* It is worth noting that, while the death penalty is prevalent in the world today, it has been abolished in a number of advanced countries, including many, such as Belgium and Italy, which are predominantly Catholic.

The revival of interest in the death penalty has been influenced to a great deal by the emergence of ''new'' crimes — airplane hijacking, political terrorism, drug pushing. These crimes help explain the emotionalism behind this support. The basic reasons behind this revival of interest are desperation, ignorance, convenience and vengeance.

Desperation. When confronted with a new situation, we usually resort to old patterns of response. Thus, it's logical to fall back on the death penalty as an answer to these crimes, but something which has failed in the past is, in this instance, bound to fail again.

Ignorance. The public is basically ignorant about the death penalty — the conventional wisdom that capital punishment prevents crime is just not borne out by the facts. The public is also generally unaware of other factors which influence attitudes toward capital punishment.

Convenience. The comment has been made that abortion fits well into the American way of life because it simply eliminates the problem — the unwanted baby. The death penalty functions the same way — we deal with the problem by excising it.

Vengeance. The often unspoken motivation behind cries for the death penalty is the base human desire for vengeance — not only to pay bloodshed with bloodshed, but with bloodshed in a tortuous, "cruel and unusual" manner.

Henry Wiehofen in **The Urge to Punish** wrote: "No one is more ferocious in demanding that the murderer or rapist 'pay' for his crime than the man who has felt strong impulses in the same direction. ...It is never he who is without sin who casts the first stone. ...A criminal trial, like a prizefight, is a public performance in which the spectators work off in a socially acceptable way aggressive impulses of much the same kind that the man on trial worked off in a socially unacceptable way."

Psychiatrist Karl Menninger has written that "just so long as the spirit of vengeance has the slightest vestige of respectability, so long as it pervades the public mind and infuses its level upon the statute books of the law, we will make no headway toward the control of crime. We cannot assess the most appropriate and effective penalties so long as we seek to inflict retaliatory pain."

A society indicates its attitudes toward life in its actions concerning war, abortion, capital punishment, suicide, and care for the aged and retarded. It is difficult to look at America's actions in these areas — particularly in the midst of the current national mood — and see a strong respect for life. This alone is enough reason to oppose capital punishment.

But when we consider the lack of "practical" justification, as well as theological and philosophical justification, we can only state with as much force as possible our opposition to the reinstatement of the death penalty, and our belief that support for the death penalty indicates an anti-life, vindictive nature inconsistent with the gospel.

DISTINGUISHING BETWEEN STATEMENTS THAT ARE PROVABLE AND THOSE THAT ARE NOT

"If the advocates of capital punishment are correct, the more people who witness executions the more effective the deterrent becomes.

"You don't get the required deterrent effect by carrying out executions behind high prison walls and steel doors; out of the public's sight. Let's end this sneaky legalized killing behind closed doors.

"Let the public see what's happening. Let them see the barbarous task society has assigned to prison officers and executioners.

"When people have had the opportunity to see what an execution is all about they'll probably reject it."

Senator John Tunney (Democrat-California) in the **National Enquirer**, October 21, 1973.

From various sources of information we are constantly confronted with statements and generalizations about social problems. In order to think clearly about these problems, it is useful if one can make a basic distinction between statements for which evidence can be found, and other statements which cannot be verified because evidence is not available, or the issue is so controversial that it cannot be definitely proved. Students should constantly be aware that social studies texts and other information often contain statements of a controversial nature. The following exercise is designed to allow you to experiment with statements that are provable and those that are not.

Part I

Instructions

Most of the following statements are taken from chapter three, some have other origins. Consider each statement carefully. Mark (P) for any statement you believe is provable, (C) for statements that are too controversial to be proved to everyone's satisfaction, and (U) for statements that are unprovable because of the lack of evidence.

P = **Provable**
C = **Too Controversial**
U = **Unprovable**

_C_ 1. If the public could witness executions they would eliminate them.

_____ 2. Some habitual criminals and mass murderers deserve to be executed.

_P_ 3. Capital punishment is an effective deterrent.

_C_ 4. Because of expensive court costs it would be cheaper for society to do away with capital punishment.

_C_ 5. Capital punishment is cruel and unusual.

_P_ 6. Capital punishment is unfair to blacks.

_U_ 7. Capital punishment unjustly denies the criminal his right to repentence and reform.

111

_____ 8. The framers of the Constitution did not intend the constitutional phrase, ''cruel and unusual punishment,'' to apply to capital punishment.

_____ 9. The Bible justifies the use of capital punishment.

_____ 10. Most countries in the world use capital punishment.

Part II

Instructions

STEP 1. The class should break into groups of four to six students.

STEP 2. Each small group should try to locate two statements that are provable and two that are not. First examine chapter two and then turn to other chapters if necessary.

STEP 3. Each group should choose a student to record its statements.

STEP 4. The class should discuss and compare the small groups' statements.

SUICIDE

Readings

THE RIGHT TO SUICIDE

Mary Rose Barrington

Mary Rose Barrington, a professional lawyer, originally intended to practice medicine. She received a degree in English from Oxford University in 1947 and in 1957 was admitted to the Bar in England. She is a member of the Executive Committee of the Euthanasia Society in England.

Consider the following questions while reading:

1. What does Ms. Barrington mean when she claims that it is not suicide that should make one shudder, but the feeling of despair that causes many suicides?
2. Why are people who would like to end their lives reluctant to do so or even talk about it with their families, friends and doctors?
3. How does the author react to doctors who would not aid a patient in ending his life?

Mary Rose Barrington, ''Apologia for Suicide,'' **Euthanasia and the Right to Die**, ed. A. B. Downing (Los Angeles: Nash Publishing, 1969), pp. 153-70. **Euthanasia and the Right to Death** edited by A. B. Downing, published by Peter Owen.

INDOCTRINATION AGAINST SUICIDE

Indoctrination against suicide is regrettably to be found at all levels. In itself the tendentious expression 'to commit suicide' is calculated to poison the unsuspecting mind with its false semantic overtones, for, apart from the dangerous practice of committing oneself to an opinion, most other things committed are, as suicide once was, criminal offences. People are futher influenced by the unhappy shadow cast over the image of suicide by the wide press coverage given to reports of suicide by students who are worried about their examinations, or girls who are upset over a love affair, or middle-aged people living alone in bed-sitting rooms who kill themselves out of depression — troubles that might all have been surmounted, given time. In pathetic cases such as these, it is not, as it seems to me, the act of suicide that is horrifying, but the extreme unhappiness that must be presumed to have induced it. Death from despair is the thing that ought to make us shudder, but the shudder is often extended to revulsion against the act of suicide that terminates the despair, an act that may be undertaken in very different circumstances. ...

People who insist that life must always be better than death often sound as if they are choosing eternal life in contrast to eternal death, when the fact is that they have no choice in the matter; it is death now, or death later. Once this fact is fully grasped it is possible for the question to arise as to whether death now would not be preferable. ...

THE NATURAL RIGHT TO DIE

Very little is 'natural' about our present-day existence, and least natural of all is the prolonged period of dying that is suffered by so many incurable patients solicitously kept alive to be killed by their disease. The sufferings of animals (other than man) are heart-rending enough, but a dying process spread over weeks, months or years seems to be one form of suffering that animals are normally spared. When severe illness strikes them they tend to stop eating, sleep and die. The whole weight of Western society forces atten-tion on the natural right to live, but throws a blanket of silence over the natural right to die. If I seem to be suggest-ing that in a civilized society suicide ought to be considered a quite proper way for a well-brought-up person to end his life (unless he has the good luck to die suddenly and without warning), that is indeed the tenor of my argument; if it is received with astonishment and incredulity, the reader is referred to the reception of recommendations made earlier in the century that birth control should be practised and encouraged. The idea is no more extraordinary, and would be equally calculated to diminish the sum total of suffering among humankind. ...

CHOOSING DEATH

Attention is here being drawn to people who unfortunately have good reason to question whether or not they want to exercise their right to live; the minor infirmities of age, and relative weakness, and a slight degree of dependence on younger people who regard the giving of a helping hand as a natural part of the life-cycle, do not give rise to any such question. The question arises when life becomes a burden rather than a pleasure.

Many middle-aged people are heard to express the fervent wish that they will not live to be pain-ridden cripples, deaf, dim-sighted or feeble-minded solitaries, such that they may become little else than a burden to themselves and to others. They say they hope they will die before any of these fates descend upon them, but they seldom affirm that they intend to die before that time; and when the time comes, it may barely cross their minds that they could, had they then the determination, take the matter into their own hands. The facile retort will often be that this merely goes to show that people do not really mean what they say and that like all normal, sensible folk, they really want to live on for as long as is physically possible. But this, I would suggest, is a false conclusion. They mean exactly what they say, but the conditions and conditioning of society make it impossible for them to act in accordance with their wishes. To face the dark reality that the future holds nothing further in the way of joy or meaningful experience, and to face the fact without making some desperate and false reservation, to take the ultimate decision and act upon it knowing that it is a gesture that can never be repeated, such clear-sightedness and resolution demand a high degree of moral strength that cannot but be undermined by the knowledge that this final act of self-discipline would be the subject of head-shakings, moralizings and general tut-tutting.

How different it would be if a person could talk over the future with his family, friends and doctors, make arrangements, say farewells, take stock of his life, and know that his decision about when and how to end his life was a matter that could be the subject of constructive and sympathetic

116

THIS DECLARATION is made

by _____

of _____

I DECLARE AS FOLLOWS:

If I should at any time suffer from a serious physical illness or impairment thought in my case to be incurable
and expected to cause me severe distress or render me
incapable of rational existence, then, unless I revoke
this declaration or express a wish contrary to its terms,
I REQUEST the administration of whatever quantity of
drugs may be required to prevent my feeling pain or
distress and, if my suffering cannot be otherwise re-
lieved, to be kept continuously unconscious at a level
where dreaming does not take place, AND
I DECLINE to receive any treatment or sustenance
designed to prolong my life.
I ASK sympathetically disposed doctors to acknowledge
the right of a patient to request certain kinds of treatment and to decline others, and I assure them that if in
any situation they think it better for me to die than to
survive, I am content to endorse their judgment in
advance and in full confidence that they will be acting
in my interests to spare me from suffering and
ignominy, and also to save my family and friends from
anguish I would not want them to endure on my behalf.

SIGNED _____

WE TESTIFY that the above named declarant signed
this declaration in our presence, and appeared to ap-
preciate its significance. We do not know of any
pressure being brought upon him/her to make a
declaration, and we believe it is made by his/her own
wish. So far as we are aware, we do not stand to benefit
by the death of the declarant.

Signed by _____

of _____

Signed by _____

of _____

conference, and even that he could have his chosen ones around him at the last. ...

VOLUNTARY EUTHANASIA

That voluntary euthanasia is in fact assisted suicide is no doubt clear to most people, but curiously enough many who would support the moral right of an incurably sick person to commit suicide will oppose his having the right to seek assistance from doctors if he is to effect his wish. ...

Hostile sections of the medical profession will continue to assert that it is their business to cure and not to kill, and that in any case a patient who is in a miserable state from having his body invaded with cancers (or whatever) is in no state to make a decision about life and death. A patient who is in so pitiable a condition that he says he wishes to die is ipso facto not in a fit condition to make a reliable statement about his wishes. Arguments of this ilk seem at times to pass from black comedy to black farce. With the same sort of metaphysical reasoning it will be maintained that a patient who requested, and was given, euthanasia on Monday evening might, had he lived until Tuesday morning, have changed his mind. It has even been suggested that patients would, if voluntary euthanasia were available for incurable patients, feel themselves reluctantly obliged to ask for it to spare the nursing staff. And, as was remarked earlier, although laying down one's life in battle is generally considered praiseworthy, to lay down your life to spare yourself pointless suffering, to release medical staff so that they can tend people who would have some chance of living enjoyable lives given greater attention and assistance, to release your family and friends from anxiety and anguish, these motives are considered shocking. More accurately, a mere contemplation of these motives shocks the conditioned mind so severly that no rational comment can fight its way through to the surface; it is forced back by the death taboo. ...

There are many more doctors who are not at all opposed in principle to suicide, but who feel, whatever the logic of the matter, that they could not personally give a patient a lethal dose. This might be regarded as the same sort of squeamishness (for lack of a better word) that would prevent another sort of person from hitting a hopelessly injured bird over the head to put it out of its suffering. He would have to waste time filling a biscuit-tin with household gas, or taking the wounded creature to a clinic, or just looking for someone less squeamish. If really cowardly he may consider putting it back in the bushes in the delusive hope that it will make a recovery. But an honest person would have to admit that it was wrong in principle to let the animal suffer because of his 'sensitive' inaction. ...

THE GIFT OF DEATH

It is, of course, all too easy to make light of death when it seems far from imminent, and all too easy for someone who has had a satisfying life to say that other people, who may have had very little happiness, must learn to accept that their one and (ostensibly) only life must now cease. It may well turn out that we who insist on the right to come to terms with death before life becomes a burden may, when the time comes, be found to fail in our resolute purpose, and may end our lives by way of punishment in one of the appalling institutions provided by the state for the care of the aged. The failure may be due to physical helplessness coupled with the refusal of others to give the necessary help, or it may be due to a moral failure ascribable to personal weakness and the pressures of society, pressures that sometimes take a form too oblique to be recognized as twisters of the mind. Ending with a further complaint about linguistic misdirection, my final objection to tainted words is that a patient ending his own life, or a doctor assisting him to end it, is said to 'take life', just as a thief 'takes' property with the intention of depriving the owner of something he values. Whatever it is that is taken from a dying patient, it is nothing he wants to keep, and the act is one of giving rather than taking. The gift is death, a gift we shall all have to receive in due course, and if we can bring ourselves to choose our time for acceptance, so much the better for us, for our family, for our friends and for society.

A CATHOLIC VIEW OF SUICIDE

Ignace Lepp

Ignace Lepp, before his death, was a psychologist, psychotherapist and Catholic priest. His book **Death and Its Mysteries**, from which this reading was taken, explores such topics as the experience of death, the death instinct, various aspects of suicide, the meaning of death and the immortality of the soul. Among other books he wrote are **Atheism in Our Time**, **The Psychology of Loving** and **The Authentic Morality**. Before his conversion to Catholicism he was a communist intellectual and taught philosophy at the University of Tiflis in Russia.

Consider the following questions while reading:

1. According to the author, what has been Christianity's position on suicide?
2. What is the author's position on suicide?

Ignace Lepp, **Death and Its Mysteries** (New York: Macmillan Company, 1968), pp. 101-05. Reprinted with permission of Macmillan Publishing Co., Inc. from **Death and Its Mysteries** by Ignace Lepp. Copyright © 1968 by Macmillan Publishing Co., Inc.

I am speaking...as a psychologist rather than a moralist. But some readers may have the impression that I consider suicide a moral evil as well as a disease to be treated by medical science. The laws of many countries in fact condemn suicide as a crime.

Individualistic moralists and philosophers do not object in principle to a person's intention to commit suicide. Since everyone lives for himself and is the master of his own life, nothing is more logical than the right to renounce that life when the individual so pleases. ...Montaigne looked upon suicide as "the pleasure of affirming one's independence from nature by taking its place. ...The most voluntary death is the most beautiful. Our life depends on the will of others; death can depend on our own will." According to Henri de Montherlant, also a great admirer of the Stoics, suicide in addition procures the superior man "the pleasure of withdrawing from the lot of the common man," who docilely submits to the law of nature. And Dostoevsky's Kirilov exclaimed, "Whoever wants supreme freedom must kill himself. He who dares to take his own life is God!"

Perhaps Christianity's fundamental anti-individualism is nowhere more manifest than in its categorical rejection of a man's right to take his own life. Almost all moralists outside of Christianity are at least tolerant with respect to suicide and often admire it. The Christian believes that life is a gift of God over which man has no proprietary rights. He is a mere depository. Christian morality admits no distinction between murder and suicide. In both cases man is infringing upon God's rights. In practice, the Church is far more lenient toward murder, many forms of which she justifies, than toward suicide. Moreover, statistics show that suicide is more prevalent in Protestant countries than in Catholic ones. The reason for this is not only that Catholicism is especially categorical in its condemnation of suicide and refuses to grant it that "romantic" admiration it often enjoys elsewhere but, more importantly, that the Catholic doctrine of the mystical body reinforces the natural social bond among men and thus rejects individualism more resolutely.

St. Thomas Aquinas based his rejection of suicide on the natural law, in much the same spirit as he tried to prove the perfect conformity of all Christian morality with the natural law. Like Aristotle, he begins with the principle that man does not belong to himself but to society, being by definition a "social animal." Suicide is a crime of homicide against society, depriving it of one of its members just as surely as if one had murdered his neighbor. On this point, Marxist morality is in perfect accord with Thomism. It does admit the legitimacy of suicide in the alienated world of capitalism, but absolutely nothing could justify it in the reconciled world of socialism. It is well known that the press in communist countries refuses to publish statistics on the number of suicides committed. A young Russian poet, taking advantage of the relative freedom that followed de-Stalinization, created something of a scandal by recalling that two of the most renowned poets of the revolution, Iessenine and Maiakovsky, committed suicide because they found the Communist regime intolerable. But St. Thomas does not argue that suicide is a crime in the name of social utilitarianism, but rather because it implies a violation of the duty of charity which every man has to himself as a creation of God.

ALL LIFE HAS MEANING

The courage to be, as expressed in Christian and Jewish thought, is more than the overcoming of the fear of death, although it includes that Stoic dimension. It is the courage to accept one's own life as having worth no matter what life may bring, including the threat of death, because that life remains meaningful and is regarded as worthy by God, regardless of what that life may be like.

Arthur J. Dyck, "An Alternative To the Ethic of Euthanasia," **To Live and To Die: When, Why, and How**, ed. Robert H. Williams (Springer-Verlag: New York, 1973) p. 106. Arthur J. Dyck is a member of the Divinity School, and member of the Center For Population Studies, Harvard University.

It is important, however, to bear in mind that the problem of man's right to commit suicide has not always been construed in such simple terms, even by Christians. Thus Paul Landsberg, a German Catholic philosopher who was killed by the Nazis in 1944, confessed that he was psychologically and philosophically disposed to consider suicide justified in certain extreme circumstances. ...In his posthumous book, **The Moral Problem of Suicide**, Landsberg writes that the only argument against the right to commit suicide seems to him the duty every Christian has to imitate Christ. All arguments against suicide from natural law fail to stand up to critical examination and in any case are unconvincing in the eyes of a man who is sufficiently motivated psychologically to do away with a life that has grown intolerable. I agree with this position. Paul Landsberg in fact underwent a cruel death because of his conviction. He had been much impressed by St. Peter's admonition: "We must not, brethren, feel suffering for Christ, since he freely gave himself up to death for our salvation." At first, Landsberg was impressed by the last part of the sentence, which seemed to him to justify the kind of suicide that is motivated, not by boredom with life, but by the courage to die voluntarily. But later, after his own spiritual outlook had matured, he saw in it an exhortation to imitate Christ. Since Christ had willingly submitted to violent death, Landsberg concluded that the Christian can imitate Christ by permitting himself to be killed by persecutors although not by killing himself.

Another philosopher of great spiritual insight, Louis Lavelle, found the idea of suicide repulsive. Since life is sacred, suicide is a "sacred crime." "The fact that one man refuses to live," he wrote, "seems to condemn all life." In my opinion, Lavelle is too severe in his judgment of suicide. It would be correct if men committed suicide in all liberty and lucidity. But we have seen that only the exceptional Stoics manage to take their lives with such a heightened awareness of what they are doing. In all other cases, the deep psychological motives for such a decision are the result of a serious inhibition of the life instinct or a crippling neurosis. Suicide represents a choice that is more or less determined.

If we could abstract from each suicide its subjective motives, I would be inclined to agree with Lavelle and Christian moralists in their categorical rejection of suicide. Whatever form it takes and under whatever conditions it happens, suicide is always an act of absolute separation from the universe and other members of the human community, a violent rupture of those relationships that are the very foundation of the human condition. He who commits suicide not only kills himself but in fact injures all life, since by his action he deprives it of his assistance. Thus, objectively, he

SUICIDE IS NOT AN INDIVIDUAL MATTER

The person who causes his or her own death repudiates the meaningfulness and worth of his or her own life. To decide to initiate an act that has as its primary purpose to end one's life is to decide that that life has no worth to anyone, especially to oneself. It is an act that ends all choices regarding what one's life and whatever is left of it is to symbolize.

Suicide is the ultimately effective way of shutting out all other people from one's life. Psychologists have observed how hostility for others can be expressed through taking one's own life. People who might want access to the dying one to make restitution, offer reparation, bestow last kindnesses, or clarify misunderstanderings are cut off by such an act. Every kind of potentially and actually meaningful contact and relation among persons is irrevocably severed except by means of memories and whatever life beyond death may offer. Certainly for those who are left behind by death, there can remain many years of suffering occasioned by that death.

Arthur J. Dyck, ''An Alternative To the Ethic of Euthanasia,'' **To Live and To Die: When, Why, and How**, ed. Robert H. Williams (Springer-Verlag: New York, 1973) pp. 106-07.

rejects human and cosmic solidarity. Those who die naturally or accidentally also deprive the community of their help and are equally separated from it. But they have no moral responsibility for their fate. This is the principal theoretical difference between natural death and suicide — and I consider accidental ''natural'' in this perspective. All death is sorrowful but suicide is tragic. ...

It seems, then, that we might offer a reasonably exact synthesis of contemporary theological, moral, sociological and psychological positions in the following manner: Suicide as such is reprehensible but we must have a great deal of understanding of and pity for the victims of suicide. The problem of suicide calls not so much for moral condemnation as for a battle against the principal causes of suicide, in particular against neurosis, loneliness and depression. The problem is, in fact, far more psychological than either sociological or moral.

AMERICAN FUNERAL PRACTICES

THE FUNERAL
WITH THE BODY PRESENT:
AN EXPERIENCE OF VALUE

Howard C. Raether and Robert C. Slater

Howard C. Raether is the Executive Director of the National Funeral Directors Association. Robert C. Slater is Professor and Director of the Mortuary Science Department at the University of Minnesota.

The following questions should help you examine the reading:

1. Why is the funeral a valuable experience?
2. What is the purpose of viewing a dead body?
3. How expensive is the average American funeral?
4. What is the role of the funeral director?

This reading was excerpted from a statement sent to the editor by the authors.

Insofar as our funerals meet...needs as they are present in the individual mourners, the funeral is an experience of value.''

Rev. Paul E. Irion, Professor of Pastoral Care at the Lancaster Theological Seminary of the United Church of Christ, said this almost twenty years ago when death truly was a taboo subject. Now that it is one of the most discussed topics of the day, it is meaningful to examine the immediate post-death customs of our culture to determine if they are only a vestige or whether they have value for those who mourn.

The Funeral Is Not of American Origin

The American funeral director did not invent the funeral. Since the beginning of recorded history, the customs of most cultures include viewing the dead body and then burying or cremating it with ceremony. In doing this, psychologists say, people confirm the reality of what has happened. The confrontation of the dead body makes it easier to realize that the dead person is no longer alive. Most bereaved persons need social support during the major separation crisis that follows death. The sorrows of the survivors also may become the sorrows of those who attend the rite or ceremony. In the appropriate setting, if the bereaved is religiously oriented, his or her faith can be affirmed by the rites, symbols and ceremonies which become a part of the funeral service. In this sense, the funeral can provide the bereaved with a proper vehicle for mourning because just as joy shared is joy increased, grief shared is grief diminished. ...

Questions and Answers About the American Funeral

Dr. Robert Fulton, Director of the Center for Death Education and Research at the University of Minnesota, explains that we in the United States today have the first death-free generation in the world. Millions of Americans have never seen a dead body except during a movie or a television show, on a highway or battle field. Few have had ''funeral experience.''...

In such a setting, it is not surprising that young and old alike have many questions about death. Here are some of the most often-asked questions and answers relating to funerals and funeral service.

NO GOOD SUBSTITUTE FOR FUNERALS

I've seen case after case of depression caused by the inability of patients — young and old — to work through their feelings after a death. I've found that people are often better off if they have a funeral to focus their feelings on. That lets them do the emotional work necessary in response to the loss. ...

I see constant evidence that the problems resulting from a serious separation — through death, divorce, or other means — can have great psychological impact. If these problems remain unresolved, grave emotional trouble can result later. ...

Are there any satisfactory funeral substitutes — a memorial service, for example? In my opinion, there aren't.

William M. Lamers, Jr. (Psychiatrist, Kentfield, California) in "Funerals Are Good For People — M.D.'s Included," **Medical Economics**, June 23, 1969.

What is a funeral?

West Coast psychiatrist Dr. William M. Lamers, Jr., says that the funeral is "an organized, purposeful, flexible, time limited, group centered response to death."...

World renowned composer-conductor Leonard Bernstein wrote an article adopted from a eulogy he gave at the funeral for singer, Jennie Tourel. The first and second paragraphs of the piece, which was in the December 9, 1973, **New York Times**, said in part:

It took me a long time to discover the values of a funeral ceremony. I had always abhorred and avoided them as pomposities — pompes funebres — and as a poor way to say goodbye, a needlessly public way of paying one's private last respects. And then, on one especially personal occasion, I suddenly discovered what everyone else had apparently known all along; that funerals are for the living, that they cause us to come together in a way we otherwise never do, to lean on one another, to feel the communality of emotions, to cry together, and — yes — to rejoice together, to rejoice in the one who has caused this coming together...

Should the body be present during the funeral?

Yes. Author and lecturer Dr. Edgar N. Jackson says:

At its best a funeral should help people face reality, express feelings and gain group support. The late Erich Lindemann, who was Professor of Psychiatry at Harvard, said that nothing helps people face reality like the moments of truth when the living confront the dead. This has in most cultures and in most times been central in the funeral process. To avoid confronting death is to pervert the purpose of the funeral and reduce its efficiency. The change of status death brings can best be faced through recognizing physical death as the basic step toward honest and healthful mourning.

What is the purpose of viewing a dead body?

Psychiatrists claim that the old adage, "seeing is believing," is useful for many bereaved people. Viewing the dead may be of greater importance today than ever before for three reasons. First, an increasing proportion of people die away from home, often in distant medical institutions, and the bereaved may not grasp death's reality without seeing the body. Second, there is an increasing proportion of deaths which follow a lingering illness, and the bereaved may have unpleasant memories of the wasted and emaciated appearance of the dying person. Third, there is an increasing proportion of people who die under tragic circumstances, and the bereaved may be unwilling to accept such a death following a tragedy. Viewing the dead body helps make those who survive more aware of the reality of death.

During a lingering illness, a person's face may be disfigured with the effects of pain or malignancy. As a result of an accident or a violent death, an entire body may be disfigured. In both instances, proper preparation and, when necessary, restoration help to modify and remove the ravages of disease or the marks of violence. Preparation, restoration and the use of cosmetics are not meant to make the dead look alive; they are intended to help provide an acceptable image for recalling the deceased.

Viewing has been found to be therapeutic for people of all ages. It may be especially helpful for a child who has experienced the death of a relative or close friend. Instead of fantasizing with a vivid imagination, with the dead body present, the child may be able to comprehend the real meaning of death.

Is it an ordeal for survivors of a death to receive people during visitation, calling hours, the wake or shivah?

No. Generally, the funeral is a ceremony to which no one is invited but all may attend. The same is true of the condolence or sympathy visit; not only is a visit appreciated, but it also is often most helpful to the bereaved.

What the visitor must overcome is the mistaken belief that the mourner prefers to be alone. Moreover, pain suffered in solitude is heavier to bear than pain which is shared. By just being there, the relative, friend or neighbor testifies to the reality of the death as well as to the support of the living community.

Whatever the participation, there is the important opportunity to express feelings and offer sympathy to the bereaved. Many times the very presence of a person speaks to the fact that life must go on, especially if that person has experienced the death of someone close. ...

Are there any important general considerations one must have in mind when considering what is to be paid for a funeral and final disposition of a body?

Yes! The funeral is usually selected by the family of the deceased. Their needs, desires and demands must be considered. Generally, their decision is rooted in religious and ethnic customs, family preferences and traditions and the customs and traditions of their community. Then, too, the economy of an area has its effect on funeral costs, just as it does on the cost of other services and commodities.

As in most "purchases," the price paid for something relates to the need for and the value in the service and/or the merchandise. In this regard, in Dr. Colin Murray Parkes' recent book, **Bereavement**, he writes: "What is the cash value of a funeral? This is a question easier to ask than to answer, for the funeral is usually regarded as a last gift..."

What statistics are available as to what a funeral costs?

Funeral costs are primarily determined by those arranging for the service.

The National Funeral Directors Association conducts an annual nationwide survey among the funeral homes or mortuaries reported to it as members to determine the average amount people pay for the funerals they select. The most recent survey indicates that in 1972 Americans paid $1,097 for the "average regular adult" funeral they selected.

In addition to regular adult funerals, there are funerals for children and indigents and partial services where death occurred other than where the funeral and/or burial was held and two funeral homes were involved or where less than a "total" or "standard" or "complete" funeral was desired. When "all services conducted" were considered, the average amount paid was $933.

Of all funeral services selected in 1972 from funeral homes participating in the study: 3.2% were priced between $200 and $499; 14% between $500 and $799; 17% between $800 and $999; 18.4% between $1,000 and $1,199; 17.9% between $1,200 and $1,499; 6.7% between $1,500 and $1,999; and 1.9% over $2,000. The remaining 20.9% in-

cluded funeral services for children, welfare recipients or partial services, i.e., less than a total funeral.

These figures do not include a vault, burial clothing, cemetery or crematorium expenses, a monument or marker, or miscellaneous items such as honorarium for the clergyman, flowers, transportation charges not included in the price of the funeral or newspaper notices. ...

Is it true that funeral directors make a big profit?

The following are facts on which the reader can base his or her answer.

In 1972 the investment range of those participating in the previously referred to study was from an average of $105,925 for funeral homes which conducted less than 100 funerals that year to $739,696 for those that had more than 300 services.

The major expense item for a funeral home is salaries. Personnel, facilities and equipment must be available twenty-four hours a day to serve the public.

The following percentages reflect expenses involved in providing the average funeral in 1972: salaries (28%); burial merchandise available from the funeral director (20%); building and occupancy (11%); cash advanced as an accommodation to the family (11%); supplies, services, collections and promotion (7%); automobile (6%); genereal expense (5%); and taxes (4%). This leaves a profit margin of 8%.

It is also interesting that the U.S. Bureau of Labor Statistics indicates that in the period between December, 1963, and April 30, 1972, all items within the Cost of Living Index has risen 41.3%. During the same period, the costs of "funeral services, adult" had risen 32.1%.

What should the basic philosophy of a funeral director be?

The philosophy of a funeral director should place the highest priority on the needs of the families which he serves. His first concern should be their mental, spiritual and physical well-being. ...

What about prearranging your own funeral in advance?

Funeral and burial arrangements are an important consideration and should be discussed openly and frankly. Prearranging and sometimes prefinancing a funeral is a method with which some people choose to assist their survivors after death occurs. However, there is no way of knowing beforehand exactly when, where, how and under what circumstances death will occur, and these unknown factors might alter original plans substantially.

Four things should be taken into consideration in planning a funeral in advance of need:

- Review the possible effect on survivors.

- Approach realistically the logic and economics of planning now what might not take place for many years.

- Keep in mind that the selection of a funeral director or a funeral firm as well as of burial merchandise, including an interment receptacle for use at a future indeterminable time, must, of necessity, be on a tentative basis.

- Monies paid in advance of need for funeral services and merchandise are governed by law in most states. Where there is no such law and monies are paid in advance, all funds should be placed in trust with the prearranger maintaining control of the account. Anyone making arrangements should be certain to have the right to terminate the contract at any time without forfeiture of any of the funds paid or earnings accrued.

Do memorial societies provide funeral services?

They do not. They have no licensed staff or facilities or equipment with which to conduct funerals. Most of the time they act as a third party between the survivors of a death and a funeral director with whom they have a contract or an understanding. This generally is done in advance of death. Contacting memorial societies immediately after death is often difficult because their telephones are not staffed twenty-four hours a day and some do not even have a phone.

What do these societies suggest and how might it affect those who follow their recommendations?

Memorial societies generally recommend immediate disposition of the body with a bodiless memorial service sometime thereafter. For most people, this is contrary to what has been learned about grief reaction. Death is a loss; and for the well-being of an individual and of society, it is important to acknowledge realistically the loss that has occurred and to give testimony to the life that has been lived. Some Americans, through the memorial society movement, attempt to sanitize their lives or intellectualize their emotions following a death by using euphemisms in their speech, disguising their behavior and sedating their emotions, as if to pretend that what has happened has, in fact, not occurred at all.

SIMPLICITY AND ECONOMY IN FUNERAL ARRANGEMENTS

the Continental Association

The Continental Association is the parent association of the numerous funeral and memorial societies in the United States. A memorial society "is a group of people who have joined together to obtain dignity, simplicity and economy in funeral arrangements by advance planning." This reading is from **A Manual of Death Education and Simple Burial**, a publication of the Continental Association.

Bring the following questions to your reading:

1. What are the negative and positive aspects of death?
2. Why is a funeral with the dead body present a negative and unworthy way to signalize death?
3. What is the purpose of a memorial society?
4. How does the Continental Association view funeral directors and the funeral industry?

Ernest Morgan, **A Manual of Death Education and Simple Burial**, 1973. Reprinted with permission from The Continental Association.

THE SIGNIFICANCE OF SIMPLE BURIAL

Because death is a universal experience, and because it almost invariably has a profound emotional and social impact on the survivors, the customs and practices associated with it are very important.

Death is both a negative and a positive experience; negative because it is the end of an individual physical life; positive because of its great potential for the maturing and deepening of the lives of the survivors. The negative aspect of death is the physical, and commonly the financial. So also, in large part but not entirely, is grief. The positive aspect of death can best be described as the spiritual.

To many religious people of all faiths, and secular-minded as well, the pre-occupation of a funeral with the dead body represents a misplacing of emphasis, no matter how thoughtful the sermon, how impressive the surroundings or how gracious the funeral director. Further, the competitive social display implicit in a "fine" funeral ("expected of the family because of its position in the community") is itself a negative and unworthy manner in which to signalize death.

A simple procedure, whereby the body is removed promptly and with dignity for immediate cremation or burial, after which one or more memorial gatherings are held, can minimize the negative aspects of death and emphasize the deeper meanings and positive values of the occasion. The economy of simple burial is not the central issue.

Even with a funeral service held in the presence of the body there is room for a wide range of procedure, varying from simple rites with a closed casket, to an elaborate ceremony in which the "restored" corpse is placed on public display.

All memorial societies and funeral directors agree that each family should be free to choose the type of funeral or memorial service which it wants, and which will best fill its needs and express its religious ideals, without pressure from any organization, business or social group. Such freedom is basic to our way of life.

This brings us to the question of advance planning and of the need for Funeral and Memorial Societies.

Q. What is a memorial society?

A. A memorial society is a group of people who have joined together to obtain dignity, simplicity and economy in funeral arrangements by advance planning.

Q. Is it run by funeral directors?

A. No, it is a people's cooperative organization that assists its members in selecting a funeral director and in getting the services they want.

Q. What happens when you join?

A. The society lets you know what kinds of funeral services are available and at what cost. You talk it over in your family and decide on your preference, then fill out forms provided by the society.

Q. How does pre-planning help at time of death?

A. In several ways:

1. You know what you want, how to get it and what it will cost. You don't have to choose a casket or negotiate for a funeral.
2. Your family understands what is being done. Simplicity will not be mistaken for miserliness or lack of respect.
3. By accepting the reality of death in advance, and by discussing it frankly, you and your family are better able to meet it when it comes.

Q. Does planning really save money?

A. The amounts vary greatly, but memorial society members usually save $500 or more on a funeral.

Q. What is the basis of these savings?

A. Simplicity. If you are not trying to demonstrate social status or compete with the neighbors, a dignified and satisfying funeral need not be costly.

Q. What is the attitude of funeral directors toward memorial societies?

A. Funeral directors generally try to give each family what it wants, expecting the family to choose service which will reflect its social and economic status. In line with their stated policy they often cooperate with memorial societies. At the same time they do have high overhead and do prefer to sell their ''best'' merchandise, whereas the societies encourage simplicity and economy. Hence funeral directors sometimes have a prejudice against memorial societies.

Q. Are funerals necessary?

A. At a time of death the survivors have important social and emotional needs which should not be ignored. A funeral is one way of meeting some of these needs.

Q. Are there other ways?

A. Yes. The body can be removed immediately after death and a memorial service held later, at approximately the same time that a funeral would have been held.

Q. What is the difference?

A. In a funeral the center of attention is the dead body; the emphasis is on death. In a memorial service the center of concern is the personality of the individual who has died, and the emphasis is on life. In addition a memorial service generally involves less expense, and can be held in a greater variety of locations.

Q. What are memorial services like?

A. They vary, taking into account the religious customs of the family and the personal relationships of the one who has died. The distinctive thing about memorial services is that they stress the ongoing qualities of the person's life rather than his death. Each service can be worked out to meet the needs and circumstances of the particular family.

THE NEED FOR PLANNING

We have, in the United States and Canada, an amazing custom of displaying dead bodies in a costly and elaborate routine. Each year, in response to this custom nearly two million American families put themselves through an emotional ordeal and spend upwards of two billions of dollars doing so.

When death occurs in a family in which there has been no planning, the survivors find themselves virtually helpless in the face of entrenched custom, and dealing with a funeral director who expects them to follow this custom. Through advance planning, however, a family can have the precedent, information and moral support needed to get the type of service it wants.

Advance planning is needed, not alone in making arrangements with funeral directors, but for working out understanding within the family. A young man killed in an accident left a widow and young children with no savings. Both husband and wife believe in simple burial, and the widow was fortunate in getting a funeral director who encouraged her to carry out her desire for a simple and economical arrangement. The young man's mother, however, though she was unable to help with the expenses, insisted on an elaborate funeral.

Since there had been no advance planning, the wife was unable to resist and not only had to endure a type of ceremony which was distressing to her, but had to face life with small children, her husband gone, and a thousand dollar funeral debt hanging over her.

To help with advance planning, non-profit and memorial societies have been formed in some 120 cities in the United States and Canada. These societies cooperate with funeral directors, sometimes by having contracts with them and sometimes by advisng their members as to which firms provide the desired service. They also furnish contacts with medical schools and eye-banks, for those who wish to leave their bodies for education or science, or their eyes for sight restoration.

With the guidance of these societies thousands of member families are now being helped to secure dignity, simplicity and economy in their funerals. ...

ABOUT FUNERAL DIRECTORS

The funeral director (don't call him an undertaker) has been the object of much unkind criticism because of his tendency to encourage ostentatious and extravagant funerals.

The fault, as a rule, lies not so much with the individual funeral director as with the unique situation of the funeral industry itself.

There are over 1,800,000 deaths each year in the United States. Divide these between the 24,000 morticians and you have only 75 funerals per year. 43% of these morticians handle as many as two per week. (LeRoy Bowman, "The American Funeral," p. 90.) The situation in Canada is much the same.

An official of the National Selected Morticians (a leading trade association of the funeral industry) remarked that 2,000 firms could handle all the funeral business in America. Even trebling his figure there are four times too many. A community which is adequately served by one bank, one printshop,and one lumber yard will commonly have several fully equipped mortuaries, all of them standing idle most of the time. A printer whose plant stands idle even half the time can hardly survive in free competition. His prices will have to be too high. How do the 43% of the morticians manage whose plants are idle over 80% of the time?

They manage because they can and do charge the overhead of days or weeks of living expense and idle plant to a single funeral. This is possible because competition does not exist in their business in the same way it does in other businesses.

Mark Twain puts it neatly, with an "undertaker" saying: "There's one thing in this world which a person don't say — 'I'll look around a little and if I can't do better I'll come back and take it.' That's a coffin. And take your poor man, and if you work him right he'll bust himself on a single layout. Or especially a woman."

High prices call for elaboration of service. Things like metal burial vaults, and caskets with innerspring mattresses make about as much sense as a fur-lined bathtub, but they help wonderfully in running up the bill. As in the case of tailfins for autos, however, it is at least as much public taste which is at fault as it is the businessman.

A MEMO TO FUNERAL DIRECTORS

A Positive Approach

The ideals of simplicity and service...shared by people of many religions and from all walks of life.

If some of us at time of death wish to have the remains of our loved ones taken promptly and quietly for simple burial, or for cremation without casket, embalming or ceremony, it is not because we are stingy or because we are lacking in sentiment. On the contrary, it is because we wish our memory image of the departed to be centered on a life in its fullness, and not on a corpse — no matter how skillfully prepared.

Memorial Meetings

It is common for those who feel as we do to have a memorial service or meeting in a private home or church or other meaningful places some days after death, and entirely apart from the body. The emphasis at this meeting is placed on the living qualities of the person, rather than on death. For different faiths such services of course take different forms.

Difficulty of Getting Desired Service

When a family with wishes of this sort seeks a mortuary at a time of death, it commonly finds an organization geared to a different type of service. To obtain the simple service it desires, the family must, in many places, haggle and be made to feel cheap. Or else it must pay for something it does not want. Few people, at a time of grief, are willing to shop around or bargain. Instead they pay for elaborate services and supplies they do not want, and undergo additional emotional stress.

Such an experience often results in a deep and lasting bitterness towards funeral directors. Witness the scores of book and magazine articles which have appeared in recent years, some scholarly and thoughtful, others harsh and indignant.

A Safety Valve

For the funeral director, memorial societies can serve as safety valves by providing a channel through which families who desire simplicity and economy at time of death may get the kind of help they want in a dignified, pre-arranged manner.

My experience with these societies indicates that, except where they encounter opposition or boycott they are not usually crusading against funeral directors, but seek to cooperate with them. They expect to pay reasonable rates for the services they want. Reputable funeral directors who have cooperated for years with the larger memorial societies report themselves well pleased with the gains they have made in good will, and with the business which has come to them through the societies.

MY OBITUARY

The purpose of this exercise is to help each student see himself more objectively by reacting to his death.

Instructions

STEP 1. Each student should write his own obituary, imagining that he died yesterday. He may use his own format, however he may find it easier to respond to the suggestions below.

STEP 2. When everyone has finished volunteers may present their obituaries to the class.

STEP 3. Repeat the process, imagining that each student's death will occur five years in the future.

Suggested Obituary Outline

Jack Doe, age 17, died yesterday from ...

He is survived by ...

His church membership was ...

Other organizations he belonged to are ...

At the time of his death he was involved in ...

At his request, services will be held at ...

Donations may be sent to his favorite charity ...

He will be remembered for ...

He will be mourned by ...

His lifetime ambitions were ...

The world will miss him because of ...

APPENDIX A

SELECTED PERIODICAL BIBLIOGRAPHY

Because most school libraries have a rather limited selection of books on death related topics, the editor has compiled a bibliography of helpful and recent periodical articles. Most school libraries have back issues of periodicals for at least a few years, and it is hoped that the following titles will be of some help to the student who wants to study problems related to death in more depth.

The student who wants to explore death in even greater detail may want to send for **A Bibliography on Death, Grief and Bereavement 1845-1973** by Robert Fulton, available from the Center for Death Education and Research, listed in appendix B. This 173 page bibliography, which sells for $6.00, covers all aspects of death in its 2,639 entries.

Walter C. Alvarez — *Death With Dignity,* **The Humanist,** September/October 1972, p. 12.

America — *Abortion and the Church,* February 10, 1973, p. 110. (editorial)

Charles H. Bayer — *Confessions of An Abortion Counselor,* **Christian Century,** May 20, 1970, p. 624.

Hugo A. Bedau — *The Issue of Capital Punishment,* **Current History,** August 1967, p. 82.

Paul Blanshard and Ed Doerr — *Is Abortion Murder?* **The Humanist,** May/June 1972, p. 8.

Richard Boeth — *Now a Right to Die?* **Newsweek,** October 29, 1973, p. 78.

Daniel Callahan — *Thinking and Experiencing,* **Christianity and Crisis,** January 8, 1973, p. 296.

Congressional Digest — January 1973 (special issue on capital punishment)

Robert M. Cooper — *Euthanasia and the Notion of Death With Dignity,* **Christian Century,** February 21, 1973, p. 225.

Jack W. Cottrell — *Abortion and the Mosaic Law,* **Christianity Today,** March 16, 1973, p. 6.

| Mary Daly | *Abortion and Sexual Caste,* **Commonweal**, February 4, 1972, p. 415. |

| Robert F. Drinan | *The Abortion Decision,* **Commonweal**, February 16, 1973, p. 438. |

| Joseph Fletcher | *The Control of Death,* **Intellectual Digest**, October 1973, p. 82. |

| Elaine Freeman | *God Committee: Life-Death Decision Concerning Infants Suffering From Meningomyelocele,* **New York Times Magazine**, May 21, 1972, p. 84. |

| Gilbert Grant | *Deciding When Death Is Better Than Life,* **Time**, July 16, 1973, p. 36. (**Time** essay) |

| Marvin Kohl | *Is the Fetus a 'Human Being'?* **The Humanist**, May/June 1972, p. 8. |

| C. Eric Lincoln | *Why I Changed My Stand on Abortion,* **Christian Century**, April 25, 1973, p. 477. |

| Daniel McGuire | *Freedom to Die,* **Commonweal**, August 11, 1972, p. 423. |

| | *Death By Chance, Death By Choice,* **Atlantic**, January 1974, p. 57. |

| Margaret Mead | *Margaret Mead Answers,* **Redbook**, July 1973, p. 33. (concerns euthanasia) |

| | *Rights to Life,* **Christianity and Crisis**, January 8, 1973, p. 288. |

| John A. Miles, Jr. | *The Wife of Onan and the Sons of Cain,* **National Review**, August 17, 1973, p. 891. (discusses abortion and social technology) |

| Robert S. Morrison | *Dying,* **Scientific American**, September 1973, p. 54. |

| **National Review** | *James Buckley: Life Amendment,* June 23, 1973, p. 667. |

| John T. Noonan, Jr. | *Raw Judicial Power,* **National Review**, March 2, 1973, p. 260. (a critique of the Supreme Court's abortion decisions) |

| J. D. O'Hara | *The Elementary Sin,* **New Republic**, August 22, 1972, p. 29. (discusses suicide) |

| Norman Podhoretz | *Beyond Z.P.G.,* **Commentary**, May 1972, p. 6. |

| William D. Poe | *Do We Need Restraint In Medicine?* **Christian Century**, September 19, 1973, p. 914. |

Frank Rizzo

Bring Back Capital Punishment, **Argosy**, September 1973, p. 38.

Scientific American

What Is Death? September 1968, p. 85.

Richard Smith

A Secular Case Against Abortion On Demand, **Commonweal**, November 12, 1971, p. 151.

Arthur J. Snider

Last Rites — Do They Bring Fear Or Reassurance? **Science Digest**, June 1969, p. 60.

Suicide and Civil Rights, **Science Digest**, January 1970, p. 54.

Hallam Tennyson

Who Shall Live? Who Shall Die? **Intellectual Digest**, March 1972, p. 52.

Time

The Death Killers, September 17, 1973, p. 94.

Implications of Mercy: Case in the Netherlands, March 5, 1973, p. 70.

Leonard J. Weber

Against the Control of Death, **Intellectual Digest**, October 1973, p. 84.

Paul Wilkes

When Do We Have the Right to Die? **Life**, January 14, 1972, p. 48.

Gordon Zahn

A Religious Pacifist Looks At Abortion, **Commonweal**, May 28, 1971, p. 279.

APPENDIX B
ORGANIZATIONS TO CONTACT

American Association of Suicidology
Department of Health
2151 Berkeley Way
Berkeley, California 94704

American Cemetery Association
250 East Broad St.
Columbus, Ohio 43215

American Civil Liberties Union
22 East 40 St.
New York, New York 10016 (for the abolition of capital
punishment)

American League to Abolish Capital Punishment
33 Mt. Vernon St.
Boston, Massachusetts 02108

American Monument Association
P.O. Box 523
Olean, New York 14760

Americans United for Life
422 Washington Building
Washington, D.C. 20005

Associated Funeral Directors Service
7405 Manchester Blvd.
St. Louis, Missouri 63143

Casket Manufacturers Association of America
708 Church St.
Evanston, Illinois 60601

Center for Death Education and Research
1167 Social Science Building
University of Minnesota
Minneapolis, Minnesota 55455

Citizens Against Legalized Murder
P.O. Box 24
New York, New York 10024 (for the abolition of capital
punishment)

Continental Association of Funeral and Memorial Societies
1828 L St. N.W.
Washington, D.C. 20036

Cremation Association of America
1620 West Belmont Ave.
Fresno, California 93701

Euthanasia Educational Council
250 West 57th St.
New York, New York 10019

Foundation of Thanatology
630 West 168th St.
New York, New York 10038

Guild of American Funeral Directors
30112 Silver Spur Blvd.
San Juan Capistrano, California 92675

Jewish Funeral Directors of America
4217 Ninth St., N.W.
Washington, D.C. 20011

International Association for Suicide Prevention
2521 West Pico Blvd.
Los Angeles, California 90006

Legal Defense and Educational Fund, Inc.
10 Columbus Circle
New York, New York 10019 (for the abolition of capital
punishment)

Memorial Society Association of Canada
5326 Ada Blvd.
Edmontom, Alberta T5W 4N7

Minnesota Citizens Concerned for Life, Inc.
4803 Nicollet Ave.
Minneapolis, Minnesota 55409 (against abortion)

Monument Builders of North America
1612 Central St.
Evanston, Illinois 60201

National Abortion and Family Planning Council
7046 Hollywood Blvd., Suite 718
Los Angeles, California 90028

National Association for the Repeal of Abortion Laws
250 W. 57th St., Room 2428
New York, New York 10019

National Association of Cemeteries
1911 North Fort Meyer Drive, Suite 409
Arlington, Virginia 22209

National Catholic Cemetery Conference
710 North River Rd.
Des Plaines, Illinois 60016

National Committee to Abolish the Federal Death Penalty
1424 16th St., N.W.
Washington, D.C. 20036

National Foundation of Funeral Services
1600-1628 Central St.
Evanston, Illinois 60201

National Funeral Directors Association
135 West Wells St.
Milwaukee, Wisconsin 53203

National Funeral Directors and Morticians Association
734 West 79th
Chicago, Illinois 60620

National Right to Life Committee, Inc.
1200 15th St., N.W., Suite 500
Washington, D.C. 20005 (against abortion)

National Save a Life League
20 W. 43rd St., Suite 706
New York, New York 10036

Planned Parenthood
810 Seventh Ave.
New York, New York 10019

Committee of Ten Million
P.O. Box 10399
Glendale, California 91290 (against abortion)

CHURCH GROUPS THAT HAVE ISSUED POSITION PAPERS ON SEVERAL OF THE TOPICS IN THIS BOOK

National Council of Churches
475 Riverside Dr.
New York, New York 10027

United States Catholic Conference
1312 Massachusetts Ave., N.W.
Washington, D.C. 20005

ACKNOWLEDGMENTS

Page

24 & 25   With permission, **Handbook On Abortion**, Wilke, Hiltz and Hayes Pub. Co., Inc.

meet
the editor

DAVID L. BENDER is a history graduate from the University of Minnesota. He also has an M.A. in government from St. Mary's University in San Antonio, Texas. He has taught social problems at the high school level and is currently working on additional volumes for the Opposing Viewpoints Series.